97 Things

Every Software Architect Should Know

97 Things

Every Software Architect Should Know

Collective Wisdom from the Experts

Edited by Richard Monson-Haefel

O'REILLY®

Beijing · Cambridge · Farnham · Köln · Sebastopol · Tokyo

97 Things Every Software Architect Should Know

Edited by Richard Monson-Haefel

Published by O'Reilly Media, Inc. 1005 Gravenstein Highway North, Sebastopol CA 95472

O'Reilly books may be purchased for educational, business, or sales promotional use. Online editions are also available for most titles (*safari.oreilly.com*). For more information, contact our corporate/institutional sales department: (800) 998-9938 or *corporate@oreilly.com*.

Editor: Mike Loukides

Series Editor: Richard Monson-Haefel

Production Editor: Rachel Monaghan

Proofreader: Rachel Monaghan

Compositor: Ron Bilodeau

Indexer: Julie Hawks

Interior Designer: Ron Bilodeau

Cover Designer: Mark Paglietti

Print History:

February 2009:   First Edition.

ISBN: 978-0-596-52269-8

Contents

Preface

SOFTWARE ARCHITECTS occupy a unique space in the world of IT. They are expected to know the technologies and software platforms on which their organizations run as well as the businesses that they serve. A great software architect needs to master both sides of the architect's coin: business and technology. This is no small challenge, and it's why this book was created.

97 Things Every Software Architect Should Know provides advice from software architects around the world on everything from how to avoid common pitfalls to how to build talented teams. It's a smorgasbord of advice from established software architects for other software architects or those who aspire to become software architects.

It's my sincere hope that this book will be a source of inspiration and guidance for software professionals everywhere. It's also my hope that software architects will use this book and its sister website to share advice and insights into what is perhaps the most challenging profession in information technology today.

This book is probably completely different from any other book you've read. It is the combined work of more than four dozen authors, all of whom donated their thoughts and advice about software architecture without compensation. It is, in a way, an open source book in the truest sense. Each author wrote his or her own contributions, those contributions were examined and edited with the author, and then the best contributions were chosen for publication. That's not much different than an open source software project where individuals contribute code rather than knowledge and wisdom.

Permissions

The licensing of each axiom is also similar to open source. Every contribution is freely available online and licensed under Creative Commons, Attribution 3, which means that you can use the individual contributions in your own work as long as you give credit to the original author. Other open source books have been tried and have, with only a few exceptions, failed. I believe that is because it's harder for individuals to contribute to a project unless it can be modularized. This book succeeds for exactly that reason: it is modularized. Each contribution is self-contained and works both in this larger collection and on its own.

How to Contact Us

Please address comments and questions concerning this book to the publisher:

> O'Reilly Media, Inc.
> 1005 Gravenstein Highway North
> Sebastopol, CA 95472
> 800-998-9938 (in the United States or Canada)
> 707-829-0515 (international or local)
> 707-829-0104 (fax)

On the web page for this book, we list errata and any additional information. You can access this page at:

> *http://www.oreilly.com/catalog/9780596522698/*

The companion website for this book, where you can find all the axioms and full-length contributor biographies, is available at:

> *http://97-things.near-time.net*

To comment or ask technical questions about this book, send email to:

> *bookquestions@oreilly.com*

For more information about our books, conferences, Resource Centers, and the O'Reilly Network, see our website at:

> *http://www.oreilly.com/*

Safari® Books Online

When you see a Safari® Books Online icon on the cover of your favorite technology book, that means the book is available online through the O'Reilly Network Safari Bookshelf.

Safari offers a solution that's better than e-books. It's a virtual library that lets you easily search thousands of top tech books, cut and paste code samples, download chapters, and find quick answers when you need the most accurate, current information. Try it for free at *http://safari.oreilly.com*.

Acknowledgments

The idea for *97 Things Every Software Architect Should Know* was not conceived in a vacuum. There are many people who deserve credit for the idea and execution. In order, I would like to thank Jay Zimmerman, who suggested that I do a presentation for the No Fluff, Just Stuff symposiums called "10 Things Every Software Architect Should Know"; Bruce Eckel, for managing the mailing list on which the idea for this book was germinated; Jeremy Meyer, for suggesting that I create a book out of what was going to be a simple slide show; Nitin Borwankar, who suggested doing a public wiki so that everyone can be involved; and the members of Bruce's mailing list who, on nothing more than a promise, chose to donate their time and contribute the first axioms to this book. I also want to thank the dozens of software architects who worked hard to contribute to this book but whose contributions are not included. It was extremely hard to choose which axioms should be a part of this work. I'm deeply grateful to everyone who contributed content, whether it was included or not.

O'Reilly deserves credit as well for listening to this idea with open ears and backing what is more or less an untested method of creating a book. O'Reilly also deserves credit for agreeing that all content will be open source (Creative Commons, Attribution 3) and that the content will be available for free to anyone on the website. People at O'Reilly I would like to thank specifically include Mike Loukides, Mike Hendrickson, Laura Painter, and Laurel Ackerman. Without your help and guidance, this project would not be possible.

We (O'Reilly and I) are developing other "97 Things" projects. The idea is to create a new and unique series that leverages the collaborative intelligence of experts in every field that is practical. Project management, software development, and data architecture are just a few of the other topics we are already pursuing.

I hope you will find the contents of this book inspiring and that you will be inspired to contribute your own axioms to future projects!

All the best!

—Richard Monson-Haefel
Series Editor, 97 Things

Don't Put Your Resume Ahead of the Requirements

Nitin Borwankar

AS ENGINEERS WE SOMETIMES RECOMMEND technologies, methodologies, and approaches for solving problems because deep down we want to have these on our resume, not because they are the best solution for the problem. Such decisions very rarely result in happy outcomes.

The best thing for your career is a long string of happy customers eager to recommend you because you did the right thing by them and for the project. This goodwill will serve you orders of magnitude better than the latest shiny object in the latest shiny language or the latest shiny paradigm. While it is important, even critical, to stay abreast of the latest trends and technologies, this should never happen at the cost of the customer. It's important to remember that you have a fiduciary duty. As an architect you have been entrusted with the well-being of your organization, and it's expected that you will avoid all conflicts of interest and give the organization your undivided loyalty. If the project isn't cutting edge or challenging enough for your current career needs, then find one that is.

If you can't do that and you are forced to be involved in such a project, then you and everyone else will be happier using the right technology for the customer rather than for your resume. It's often difficult to resist utilizing a solution that is new and cool, even when it's inappropriate for the current situation.

With the right solution, the project will have a happier team, a happier customer, and far less stress overall. This will often give you time to go deeper into the existing older technology or to learn the new stuff on your own time. Or to go take that painting class you always wanted to. Your family will love you for it, too—they'll notice the difference when you get home.

Always put the customer's long-term needs ahead of your own short-term needs and you won't go wrong.

Nitin Borwankar worked at Ingres and Sybase in the early 1990s. He was involved with some of the earliest web-database applications using SybPerl and OraPerl, and soon after with early Enterprise Java. He was also an active participant in New-EDI, an IETF standards process for EDI on the Internet. He has been an independent consultant and researcher since 1994 and has focused on enterprise data and integration along with messaging. His current interests include database schemas for tagging (folksonomy) applications in the enterprise and database issues underlying social networks with applications in the enterprise. He is a member of the Policy Group in the Data Portability effort, where he is tasked with creating the first drafts for EULA templates that respect user data rights. He has written about database issues for GigaOm.com and blogs at http://tagschema.com. He holds a patent in messaging for collaboration across trust boundaries.

Simplify Essential Complexity; Diminish Accidental Complexity

Neal Ford

ESSENTIAL COMPLEXITY REPRESENTS the difficulty inherent in any problem. For example, coordinating a nation's air traffic is an inherently complex problem. Every plane's exact position (including altitude), speed, direction, and destination must be tracked in real time to prevent mid-air and runway collisions. The flight schedules of aircraft must be managed to avoid airport congestion in a continuously changing environment—a severe change in weather throws the entire schedule out of whack.

Conversely, accidental complexity grows from the things we feel we must build to mitigate essential complexity. The antiquated air traffic control system used today is an example of accidental complexity. It was designed to address the essential complexity of controlling the traffic of thousands of airplanes, but the solution itself introduces its own complexity. In fact, the air traffic control system used today is so complex that updating it has proven difficult, if not impossible. In much of the world, air traffic is guided by technology that is more than 30 years old.

Many frameworks and vendor "solutions" are the symptoms of the accidental complexity disease. Frameworks that solve specific problems are useful. Over-engineered frameworks add more complexity than they relieve.

Developers are drawn to complexity like moths to a flame—frequently with the same result. Puzzle solving is fun, and developers are problem solvers.

Who doesn't like the rush of solving some incredibly complex problem? In large-scale software, though, removing accidental complexity while retaining the solution to the essential complexity is challenging.

How do you do this? Prefer frameworks derived from working code rather than ones cast down from ivory towers. Look at the percentage of code you have in a solution that directly addresses the business problem versus code that merely services the boundary between the application and the users. Cast a wary eye on vendor-driven solutions. They may not be inherently bad, but vendors often push accidental complexity. Make sure that the solution fits the problem.

It's the duty of the architect to solve the problems inherent in essential complexity without introducing accidental complexity.

Neal Ford is a software architect and meme wrangler at ThoughtWorks, a global IT consultancy with an exclusive focus on end-to-end software development and delivery. He is the designer/developer of applications, instructional materials, magazine articles, courseware, and video/DVD presentations, and he is author and/or editor of five books. He also speaks at lots of conferences. You can assuage your ravenous curiosity about Neal at http://www.nealford.com.

Chances Are, Your Biggest Problem Isn't Technical

Mark Ramm

RIGHT NOW SOMEONE'S RUNNING a failing project to build a payroll system. Probably more than one someone.

Why? Was it because they chose Ruby over Java, or Python over Smalltalk? Or because they decided to use Postgres rather than Oracle? Or did they choose Windows when they should have chosen Linux? We've all seen technology take the fall for failed projects. But what are the chances that the problem was really so difficult to solve that Java wasn't up the the task?

Most projects are built by people, and those people are the foundation for success and failure. So, it pays to think about what it takes to help make those people successful.

Equally, there's a good chance that there's someone who you think is "just not doing it right" and is undermining the project. In these cases, the technology you need to solve your problem is very old and well established indeed; in fact, it's possibly the most important technical innovation in the history of humanity. What you need is a *conversation*.

Mere familiarity with the conversation as a technology isn't enough. Learning to treat people with respect, and learning give them the benefit of the doubt, is one of the core skills that turn a smart architect into an effective one.

There's lots more to it than this, but a couple of small tips can significantly increase your conversational effectiveness:

- Approach these events as conversations—not as confrontations.

  If you assume the best about people and treat this situation as an opportunity to ask questions, you definitely learn more, and are less likely to put people on the defensive.

- Approach these conversations only after you've got your attitude right.

  If you're angry, frustrated, annoyed, or otherwise flustered, it's very likely that the other person will interpret your nonverbals as an indication that you're on the attack.

- Use these as opportunities to set mutually agreed-upon goals.

  Instead of telling a developer that they need to be quiet in meetings because they never let anybody speak, ask if they can help you increase other people's participation. Explain that some people are more introverted and need longer silences before they enter into a conversation, and ask the developer to help you out by waiting five seconds before jumping in.

If you start with a shared purpose, treat people "problems" as an opportunity to learn, and manage your own emotions, you'll not only become more effective, you'll also discover that you learn something every time.

> *Mark Ramm is BDFL for TurboGears 2, a python enthusiast, and a generally crazy dude. He's done nearly every job imaginable from software architect to network administrator to lobster-trap thrower and biker-bar cleaner. He is passionate about making tools that help professional and amateur programmers more productive.*

Communication Is King; Clarity and Leadership, Its Humble Servants

Mark Richards

ALL TOO OFTEN, SOFTWARE ARCHITECTS sit in their ivory towers, dictating specifications, technology decisions, and technology direction to the developers below. More often than not, this leads to dissension in the ranks, quickly followed by a revolt by the masses, finally resulting in a software product that doesn't even come close to resembling the original requirements. Every software architect should know how to communicate the goals and objectives of a software project. The key to effective communication is clarity and leadership.

Clarity describes how you communicate. No one on your team is going to read a 100-page architecture decisions document. Being clear and concise in the way you communicate your ideas is vital to the success of any software project. Keep things as simple as possible at the start of a project, and by all means do not start writing lengthy Word documents. Use tools like Visio to create simple diagrams to convey your thoughts. Keep them simple, for they will almost certainly be changing frequently. Another effective means of communication is informal whiteboard meetings. Nothing gets your ideas across better than bringing a group of developers (or other architects) into a room and whiteboarding your ideas. Also, be sure to have a digital camera with you at all times. Nothing is more frustrating than being pushed out of a meeting room with all of your ideas stuck on a whiteboard. Snap a picture, download it, and share it via a wiki with the rest of the team. Throw away the lengthy Word documents and focus more on getting your ideas across, and afterward worry about recording the details of your architectural decisions.

One thing most software architects fail to realize is that a software architect is also a leader. As a leader, you must gain the respect of your co-workers to work in a healthy and effective environment. Keeping developers in the dark about the big picture or why decisions were made is a clear recipe for disaster. Having the developer on your side creates a collaborative environment whereby decisions you make as an architect are validated. In turn, you get buy-in from developers by keeping them involved in the architecture process. Work with developers, not against them. Keep in mind that all team members (e.g., the QA team, business analysts, and project managers, as well as developers) require clear communication and leadership. Employing clarity and demonstrating effective leadership will improve communication and create a strong and healthy work environment.

If "Communication Is King," then clarity and leadership are its humble servants.

> *Mark Richards is a director and senior solutions architect at Collaborative Consulting, LLC, where he is involved in the architecture and design of large-scale service-oriented architectures in J2EE and other technologies, primarily in the financial services industry. He has been involved in the software industry since 1984, and has significant experience in J2EE architecture and development, object-oriented design and development, and systems integration.*

Application Architecture Determines Application Performance

Randy Stafford

APPLICATION ARCHITECTURE DETERMINES application performance. That might seem rather obvious, but real-world experience shows that it's not. For example, software architects frequently believe that simply switching from one brand of software infrastructure to another will be sufficient to solve an application's performance challenges. Such beliefs may be based on a vendor's benchmark trumpeting, say, 25% better performance than the closest competition's. But if the vendor's product performs an operation in three milliseconds while the competition's product takes four milliseconds, the 25% or one-millisecond advantage matters little in the context of a highly inefficient architecture at the root of an application's performance characteristics.

In addition to IT managers and vendor benchmarking teams, other groups of people—vendor support departments and authors of application performance management literature—recommend simply "tuning" the software infrastructure, by fiddling with memory allocations, connection pool sizes, thread pool sizes, and the like. But if the deployment of an application is insufficiently architected for the expected load, or if the application's functional architecture is too inefficient in its utilization of computing resources, then no amount of "tuning" will bring about the desired performance and scalability characteristics. Instead, a re-architecting of internal logic or deployment strategy, or both, will be required.

In the end, all vendor products and application architectures are constrained by the same fundamental principles of distributed computing and underlying physics: applications, and the products they use, run as processes on computers of limited capacity, communicating with one another via protocol stacks and links of nonzero latency. Therefore people need to appreciate that application architecture is the primary determinant of application performance and scalability. Those quality attributes cannot be miraculously improved with some silver-bullet switch of software brands, or infrastructure "tuning." Instead, improvements in those areas require the hard work of carefully considered (re-)architecting.

Randy Stafford is a practicing software professional with 20 years' experience as a developer, analyst, architect, manager, consultant, and author/presenter.

Currently for Oracle's middleware development A-Team, he engages globally for proof-of-concept projects, architecture reviews, and production crises with diverse customer organizations, specializing in grid, SOA, performance, HA, and JEE/ORM work.

Seek the Value in Requested Capabilities

Einar Landre

OFTEN CUSTOMERS AND END USERS state what they think is a viable solution to a problem as a requirement. The classic story on this was told by Harry Hillaker, the lead designer of the F-16 Falcon. His team was asked to design a Mach 2–2.5 aircraft, which was then, and probably still is, a nontrivial task—especially when the objective is to create a "cheap" lightweight aircraft. Consider that the force required to overcome drag quadruples when doubling the speed, and what impact that has on aircraft weight.

When the design team asked the Air Force why it needed Mach 2–2.5, the answer was "to be able to escape from combat." With the real need on the table, the design team was able to address the root problem and provide a working solution: an agile aircraft with a high thrust-to-weight ratio, providing acceleration and maneuverability, not maximum speed.

This lesson should be brought into software development as well. By asking for the intended value of a requested feature or requirement, architects are able to address the real problem, and hopefully provide a better and cheaper solution than that suggested by the client. The focus on value also simplifies prioritization: the most valuable requirements become the driving requirements.

So, how to proceed then? In many ways the required approach is found in the agile manifesto: "Collaboration over contract." Practically speaking, this implies arranging workshops and meetings where the architects' focus is on customer needs—helping the customers to answer the "why" question. Be aware that answering the "why" question can be difficult because we very often talk about tacit knowledge. Discussions on how to provide a technical solution should be avoided in these workshops, because they move the focus away from the customer's domain and into the domain of software development.

> *Einar Landre is a practicing software professional with 25 years' experience as a developer, architect, manager, consultant, and author/presenter.*
>
> *Currently for StatoilHydro's Business Application Services, he engages in business-critical application development, architecture reviews, and software process improvement activities, specializing in SOA, domain-driven design, use of multi-agents and design of large-scale, networked, software-intensive systems.*

Stand Up!

Udi Dahan

AS ARCHITECTS, MANY OF US HAVE GROWN from highly technical positions where our success was derived mainly from our ability to talk to machines. However, in the role of architect much of our communication is now done with our fellow human beings. Whether it's talking to developers about the benefits of employing a specific pattern, or explaining to management the cost-benefit tradeoffs of buying middleware, communication is core to our success.

Although it's difficult to measure an architect's impact on a project, this much is clear: if developers consistently ignore an architect's guidance and management doesn't buy in to his recommendations, the "rightness" of his guidance will do little to advance his career. Experienced architects understand that they need to "sell" their ideas and need to communicate effectively in order to do that.

Many books have been written on the topic of interpersonal communication, but I wanted to call out one simple, practical, easy-to-employ tip that will drastically increase the effectiveness of your communication, and, consequently, your success as an architect. If you're in any situation where you're talking to more than one person about your guidance, stand up. Whether it's a formal design review, or an informal discussion over some diagrams, it doesn't matter. Stand up, especially if everyone else is sitting down.

Standing up automatically communicates authority and self-confidence. You command the room. People will interrupt you less. All that is going to make a big difference to whether or not your recommendations will be adopted.

You'll also notice that once you stand, you'll start making more use of your hands and other body language. When speaking to groups of 10 or more people, standing up will also help you make eye contact with everybody. Eye contact, body language, and other visual elements account for a large portion of communication. Standing up also tends to change your tone of voice, volume, pitch, and speed: projecting your voice to larger rooms, slowing down to make more important points. These vocal elements contribute substantially to the effectiveness of communication.

The easiest way to more than double your effectiveness when communicating ideas is quite simply to stand up.

Udi Dahan is The Software Simplist, recognized by Microsoft Corporation with the coveted Most Valuable Professional award for Solutions Architecture now three years running. Udi is a connected technologies advisor working with Microsoft on WCF, WF, and Oslo. He also serves on the Advisory Boards of the Microsoft Software Factories Initiative and the Patterns & Practices' Prism Project. He provides clients all over the world with training, mentoring, and high-end architecture consulting services, specializing in service-oriented, scalable, and secure .NET architecture design.

Everything Will Ultimately Fail

Michael Nygard

HARDWARE IS FALLIBLE, SO WE ADD REDUNDANCY. This allows us to survive individual hardware failures, but increases the likelihood of having at least one failure present at any given time.

Software is fallible. Our applications are made of software, so they're vulnerable to failures. We add monitoring to tell us when the applications fail, but that monitoring is made of more software, so it too is fallible.

Humans make mistakes; we are fallible also. So, we automate actions, diagnostics, and processes. Automation removes the chance for an error of commission, but increases the chance of an error of omission. No automated system can respond to the same range of situations that a human can.

Therefore, we add monitoring to the automation. More software, more opportunities for failures.

Networks are built out of hardware, software, and very long wires. Therefore, networks are fallible. Even when they work, they are unpredictable because the state space of a large network is, for all practical purposes, infinite. Individual components may act deterministically, but still produce essentially chaotic behavior.

Every safety mechanism we employ to mitigate one kind of failure adds new failure modes. We add clustering software to move applications from a failed server to a healthy one, but now we risk "split-brain syndrome" if the cluster's network acts up.

It's worth remembering that the Three Mile Island accident was largely caused by a pressure relief value—a safety mechanism meant to prevent certain types of overpressure failures.

So, faced with the certainty of failure in our systems, what can we do about it?

Accept that, no matter what, your system will have a variety of failure modes. Deny that inevitability, and you lose your power to control and contain them. Once you accept that failures will happen, you have the ability to design your system's reaction to specific failures. Just as auto engineers create crumple zones—areas designed to protect passengers by failing first—you can create safe failure modes that contain the damage and protect the rest of the system.

If you do not design your failure modes, then you will get whatever unpredict-able—and usually dangerous—ones happen to emerge.

Michael Nygard wrote Release It! Design and Deploy Production-Ready Soft-ware *(Pragmatic Bookshelf), which won a Jolt Productivity award in 2008. His other writings can be found at http://www.michaelnygard.com/blog.*

You're Negotiating More Often Than You Think

Michael Nygard

WE'VE ALL BEEN HIT WITH BUDGETECTURE. That's when sound technology choices go out the window in favor of cost-cutting. The conversation goes something like this.

"Do we really need X?" asks the project sponsor.

For "X", you can substitute nearly anything that's vitally necessary to make the system run: software licenses, redundant servers, offsite backups, or power supplies. It's always asked with a sort of paternalistic tone, as though the grown-up has caught us blowing all our pocket money on comic books and bubble gum, while the serious adults are trying to get on with buying more buckets to carry their profits around in.

The correct way to answer this is "Yes. We do." That's almost never the response.

After all, we're trained as engineers, and engineering is all about making trade-offs. We know good and well that you don't really need extravagances like power supplies, so long as there's a sufficient supply of hamster wheels and cheap interns in the data center. So instead of saying, "Yes. We do," we say something like, "Well, you could do without a second server, provided you're willing to accept downtime for routine maintenance and whenever a parity bit flips, causing a crash, but if we get error-checking parity memory then we get around that, so we just have to worry about the operating system crashing, which it does about every three-point-nine days, so we'll have to do nightly restart. The interns can do that whenever they get a break from the power-generating hamster wheels."

All of which might be completely true, but is utterly the wrong thing to say. The sponsor stopped listening right after the word "Well."

The problem is that you see your part as an engineering role, while your sponsor clearly understands he's engaged in a negotiation. We're looking for a collaborative solution-finding exercise; they're looking for a win-lose tactical maneuver. And in a negotiation, the last thing you want to do is make concessions on the first demand. In fact, the right response to the "do we really need" question is something like this:

"Without a second server, the whole system will come crashing down at least three times daily, particularly when it's under heaviest load or when you are doing a demo for the Board of Directors. In fact, we really need four servers so we can take one HA pair down independently at any time while still maintaining 100% of our capacity, even in case one of the remaining pair crashes unexpectedly."

Of course, we both know you don't really need the third and fourth servers. This is a counter-negotiating gambit to get the sponsor to change the subject to something else. You're upping the ante and showing that you're already running at the bare, dangerous, nearly irresponsible minimum tolerable configuration. And besides, if you do actually get the extra servers, you can certainly use one to make your QA environment match production, and the other will make a great build box.

Author bio available on page 17.

Quantify

Keith Braithwaite

"FAST" IS NOT A REQUIREMENT. Neither is "responsive." Nor "extensible." The primary reason why not is that you have no objective way to tell if they're met. But still users want them. The architect's role is largely to help the system have these qualities, and to balance the inevitable conflicts and inconsistencies between them. Without objective criteria, architects are at the mercy of capricious users ("no, I won't accept it, still not fast enough") and of obsessive programmers ("no, I won't release it, still not fast enough").

As with all requirements, we seek to write down these desires. Too often then the vague adjectives come out: "flexible," "maintainable," and the rest. It turns out that in every case (yes, even "usable," with effort), these phenomena can be quantified and thresholds set. If this is not done, then there is no basis for acceptance of the system by its users, valuable guidance is stolen from its builders as they work, and the vision is blurred for those architecting it.

Some simple questions to ask: How many? In what period? How often? How soon? Increasing or decreasing? At what rate? If these questions cannot be answered, then the need is not understood. The answers should be in the business case for the system and if they are not, then some hard thinking needs to be done. If you work as an architect and the business hasn't (or won't) tell you these numbers, ask yourself why not. Then go get them. The next time someone tells you that a system needs to be "scalable," ask that person where new users are going to come from and why. Ask how many and by when? Reject "Lots" and "soon" as answers.

Uncertain quantitative criteria must be given as a range: the least, the nominal, and the most. If this range cannot be given, then the required behavior is not understood. As an architecture unfolds, it can be checked against these criteria to see if it is (still) in tolerance. As the performance against some criteria drifts over time, valuable feedback is obtained. Finding these ranges and checking against them is a time-consuming and expensive business. If no one cares enough about the system being "performant" (neither a requirement nor a word) to pay for performance trials, then more than likely performance doesn't matter. You are then free to focus your architectural efforts on aspects of the system that are worth paying for.

"Must respond to user input in no more than 1,500 milliseconds. Under normal load (defined as…), the average response time must be between 750 and 1,250 milliseconds. Response times less than 500 milliseconds can't be distinguished by the user, so we won't pay to go below that." *Now that's a requirement.*

After many years as an amateur, Keith Braithwaite was first paid to write software in 1996. After that first job, maintaining a compiler built with lex and yacc, he progressed first to modelling microwave propagation for GSM network planning, then seasonal variations in demand for air freight, in C++. A move to consultancy (and Java) introduced him to CORBA and then EJB, and then what was called at the time "e-commerce." He is currently a principal consultant with Zuhlke and manages its Centre of Agile Practice.

One Line of Working Code Is Worth 500 of Specification

Allison Randal

DESIGN IS A BEAUTIFUL THING. A systematic, detailed presentation and review of a problem space and solution reveals errors and opportunities for improvement, sometimes in a startlingly dramatic way. The specifications are important because they provide the pattern for building. Taking the time to think through the architecture is important, both on a macro level with an eye for interactions between components and, on a micro level with an eye for behavior within a component.

Unfortunately it's far too easy to get wrapped up in the process of design, enthralled by architecture in abstract. The fact is that specifications alone have no value. The ultimate goal of a software project is a production system. A software architect must always keep an eye on this goal, and remember that design is merely a means to an end, not an end in itself. An architect for a skyscraper who ignored the laws of physics to make the building more beautiful would soon regret it. Losing sight of the goal of working code spells serious trouble for any project.

Value the team members who work on implementing your vision. Listen to them. When they have problems with the design, there's a good chance they're right and the design is wrong, or at least unclear. It's your job, in these cases, to modify the design to meet real-world constraints by working with your team members to determine what works and what does not. No design is perfect from the start; all designs need to be modified as they are implemented.

If you're also a developer on the project, value the time you spend writing code, and don't believe anyone who tells you it's a distraction from your work as architect. Your vision of both macro and micro levels will be greatly enhanced by the time you spend in the belly of the beast bringing it to life.

> *Allison Randal is chief architect and lead developer of the open source project Parrot. In more than 25 years as a programmer, she has developed everything from games to linguistic analysis tools, e-commerce websites, shipping fulfillment, compilers, and database replication systems; worked as a language designer, project manager, conference organizer, editor, and consultant; been president of an open source software foundation; written two books; and founded a tech publishing company.*

There Is No One-Size-Fits-All Solution

Randy Stafford

ARCHITECTS MUST CONTINUOUSLY develop and exercise "contextual sense"—because there is no one-size-fits-all solution to problems that may be widely diverse.

The incisive phrase "contextual sense" was coined, and its meaning insightfully described, by Eberhardt Rechtin in his 1991 book *Systems Architecting: Creating & Building Complex Systems* (Prentice Hall):

> [The central ideas of the 'heuristic approach' to architecting complex systems] come from asking skilled architects what they do when confronted with highly complex problems. The skilled architect and designer would most likely answer, 'Just use common sense.' ... [A] better expression than 'common sense' is contextual sense—a knowledge of what is reasonable within a given context. Practicing architects through education, experience, and examples accumulate a considerable body of contextual sense by the time they're entrusted with solving a system-level problem—typically 10 years." (emphasis in the original)

A big problem in the software industry, in my opinion, is that people are often responsible for solving problems requiring more contextual sense than they've accumulated. Perhaps this is because the software industry is barely two generations old and growing explosively; perhaps it will be a sign of maturity in the software industry when this problem no longer exists.

I encounter examples of this problem frequently in my consulting engagements. Typical examples include failure to apply domain-driven design[1] when appropriate, straying from a pragmatic outlook and over-designing a software solution for the essential need at hand, and making irrelevant or unreasonable suggestions during performance optimization crises.

The most important knowledge of software patterns is the knowledge of when to apply them and when not to apply them, and the same is true of different root cause hypotheses and associated corrective actions during problem analysis. In both activities—system architecting and problem analysis—it is axiomatic that there is no one-size-fits-all solution; architects must develop and exercise contextual sense in formulating and troubleshooting their architectures.

Author bio available on page 11.

---

1 See Eric Evans's *Domain-Driven Design: Tackling Complexity in the Heart of Software* (Addison-Wesley Professional).

It's Never Too Early to Think About Performance

Rebecca Parsons

BUSINESS USERS SPECIFY THEIR NEEDS primarily through functional requirements. The nonfunctional aspects of the systems, like performance, resiliency, up-time, support needs, and the like, are the purview of the architect. However, often the preliminary testing of nonfunctional requirements is left until very late in the development cycle, and is sometimes delegated completely to the operations team. This is a mistake that is made far too often.

The reasons are varied. There is presumably no sense in making something fast and resilient if it doesn't actually perform the required function. The environments and tests themselves are complex. Perhaps the early versions of the production system will not be as heavily utilized.

However, if you aren't looking at performance until late in the project cycle, you have lost an incredible amount of information as to when performance changed. If performance is going to be an important architectural and design criterion, then performance testing should begin as soon as possible. If you are using an Agile methodology based on two-week iterations, I'd say performance testing should be included in the process no later than the third iteration.

Why is this so important? The biggest reason is that at the very least you know the kinds of changes that made performance fall off a cliff. Instead of having to think about the entire architecture when you encounter performance problems, you can focus on the most recent changes. Doing performance testing early and often provides you with a narrow range of changes on which to focus.

In early testing, you may not even try to diagnose performance, but you do have a baseline of performance figures to work from. This trend data provides vital information in diagnosing the source of performance issues and resolving them.

This approach also allows for the architectural and design choices to be validated against the actual performance requirements. Particularly for systems with stringent requirements, early validation is crucial to delivering the system in a timely fashion.

Technical testing is also notoriously difficult to get going. Setting up appropriate environments, generating the proper data sets, and defining the necessary test cases all take a lot of time. By addressing performance testing early, you can establish your test environment incrementally, thereby avoiding much more expensive efforts once you discover performance issues.

> *Dr. Rebecca Parsons is ThoughtWorks' chief technology officer. She has more than 20 years' application development experience, in industries ranging from telecommunications to emergent Internet services. Rebecca has published in both language and artificial intelligence publications, served on numerous program committees, and reviews for several journals. She has extensive experience leading in the creation of large-scale distributed object applications and the integration of disparate systems.*

Architecting Is About Balancing

Randy Stafford

Balance Stakeholders' Interests with Technical Requirements

WHEN WE THINK OF ARCHITECTING SOFTWARE, we tend to think first of classical technical activities, like modularizing systems, defining interfaces, allocating responsibility, applying patterns, and optimizing performance. Architects also need to consider security, usability, supportability, release management, and deployment options, among other things. But these technical and procedural issues must be balanced with the needs of stakeholders and their interests. Taking a "stakeholders and interests" approach in requirements analysis is an excellent way to ensure completeness of requirements specifications for the software being developed.

Analyzing the stakeholders and their interests in the process by which an organization develops software, and in the organization itself, reveals the ultimate set of priorities bearing on a software architect. Software architecting is about balancing this set of priorities, over the short and long term, in a way that is appropriate to the context at hand.

Consider, for example, the engineering department of a software-as-a-service business. The business likely has certain priorities, such as meeting contractual obligations, generating revenue, ensuring customer referenceability, containing costs, and creating valuable technology assets. These business priorities may translate to departmental priorities like ensuring the functionality, correctness, and "quality attributes" (i.e., "-ilities") of the software being developed, as well as ensuring the productivity of the development team, the sustainability and auditability of development operations, and the adaptability and longevity of the software products.

It is the architect's job to not only create functional, quality software for users, but also to do so while balancing the other departmental priorities with the cost-containment interests of the business's CEO, with the ease-of-administration interests of the operations staff, with the ease-of-learning and ease-of-maintenance interests of future programming staff, and with the best practices of the software architect's profession.

The architect may choose to consciously tilt the balance in favor of one priority in the short term, but had better maintain a proper balance over the long term in order to truly do the job well. And the balance that is struck needs to be appropriate to the context at hand, in consideration of factors such as the expected lifespan of the software, the criticality of the software to the business, and the technological and financial culture of the organization.

In summary, software architecting is about more than just the classical technical activities; it is about balancing technical requirements with the business requirements of stakeholders in the project.

Author bio available on page 11.

Commit-and-Run Is a Crime

Niclas Nilsson

IT'S LATE IN THE AFTERNOON. The team is churning out the last pieces of the new feature set for the iteration, and you can almost feel the rhythm in the room. John is in a bit of a hurry though. He's late for a date, but he manages to finish up his code, compile, and check in, and off he goes. A few minutes later, the red light turns on. The build is broken. John didn't have time to run the automated tests, so he made a commit-and-run and thereby left everybody else hanging. The situation is now changed and the rhythm is lost. Everyone now knows that if they do an update against the version control system, they will get the broken code onto their local machine as well, and since the team has a lot to integrate this afternoon to prepare for the upcoming demo, this is quite a disruption. John effectively put the team flow to a halt because now no integration can be done before someone takes the time to revert his changes.

This scenario is way too common. Commit-and-run is a crime because it kills flow. It's one of the most common ways for a developer to try to save time for himself, and it ends up wasting other people's time and is downright disrespectful. Still, it happens everywhere. Why? Usually because it takes too long to build the system properly or to run the tests.

This is where you, the architect, come into play. If you've put a lot of effort into creating a flexible architecture where people can perform, taught the developers agile practices like test-driven development, and set up a continuous integration server, then you also want to nurture a culture where it's not all right to waste anybody else's time and flow in any way. To be able to get that, you need to make sure the system, among other things, has a sound architecture for automated testing, since it will change the behavior of the developers. If tests run fast, developers will run them more often, which itself is a good thing, but it also means that they won't leave their colleagues with broken code. If the tests are dependent on external systems or if they need to hit the database, re-engineer them so they can be run locally with mocks or stubs, or at the very least with an in-memory database, and let the build server run them in the slow way. People should not have to wait for computers, because if they have to, they will take shortcuts, which often causes problems for others instead.

Invest time in making the system fast to work with. It increases flow, lessens the reasons for working in silos, and in the end makes it possible to develop faster. Mock things, create simulators, lessen dependencies, divide the system in smaller modules, or do whatever you have to. Just make sure there's no reason to even think about doing a commit-and-run.

> *Niclas Nilsson is a software development coach, consultant, educator, and writer with a deep passion for the software development craft, and he loves good design and architecture. He is a cofounder of factor10 and the lead editor of the architecture community at InfoQ.*

There Can Be
More Than One

Keith Braithwaite

IT SEEMS TO BE A NEVERENDING SOURCE of surprise and distress to system builders that one data model, one message format, one message transport—in fact, exactly one of any major architectural component, policy, or stance—won't serve all parts of the business equally well. Of course: an enterprise ("enterprise" is red flag #1) big enough to worry about how many different "Account" tables will impact system building next decade is most likely too big and diverse for one "Account" table to do the job anyway.

In technical domains we can force uniqueness. Very convenient for us. In business domains the inconsistent, multifaceted, fuzzy, messy world intrudes. Worse yet, business doesn't even deal with "the world," it deals with people's opinions about aspects of situations in parts of the world. One response is to deem the domain to be technical and apply a unique solution by fiat. But reality has been roughly defined as "that which does not go away when one stops believing in it" (Philip K. Dick), and the messiness always returns as the business evolves. Thus are born enterprise data teams, and so forth, who spend all their (very expensive) time trying to tame existential dread through DTD wrangling. Paying customers tend to find the level of responsiveness that comes from this somewhat unsatisfactory.

Why not face up to the reality of a messy world and allow multiple, inconsistent, overlapping representations, services, solutions? As technologists we recoil in horror from this. We imagine terrifying scenarios: inconsistent updates, maintenance overhead, spaghetti-plates of dependencies to manage. But let's take a hint from the world of data warehousing. The schemata data marts are often (relationally) denormalized, mix imported and calculated values arbitrarily, and present a very different view of the data than the underlying databases. And the sky does not fall because of the nonfunctional properties of a mart. The ETL process sits at the boundary of two very different worlds, typically transaction versus analytical processing. These have very different rates of update and query, very different throughput, different rates of change of design, perhaps very different volumes. This is the key: sufficiently different nonfunctional properties of a subsystem create a boundary across which managing inconsistent representations is tractable.

Don't go duplicating representations, or having multiple transports just for the fun of it, but do always consider the possibility that decomposition of your system by nonfunctional parameters may reveal opportunities to allow diverse solutions to your customers' advantage.

Author bio available on page 21.

Business Drives

Dave Muirhead

IN THE CONTEXT OF BUSINESS ENTERPRISE application development, an architect must act as a bridge between the business and technology communities of an organization, representing and protecting the interests of each party to the other, often mediating between the two, but allowing the business to drive. The business organization's objectives and operating realities should be the light in which an architect leads technology-oriented decision making.

Businesses routinely plan for and articulate a specific, desired return on investment (ROI) before undertaking a software development initiative. The architect must understand the desired ROI, and by implication, the limits of the value of the software initiative to the business, so as to avoid making technology decisions that could cause the opportunity to be outspent. ROI should serve as a major piece of objective context in the give-and-take conversations with the business about the value of a feature versus the cost of delivering that feature, and with the development team about technical design and implementation. For example, the architect must be careful to represent the interests of the business to the development team by not agreeing to choose technology that has unacceptably costly licensing and support cost implications when the software is deployed into testing or production.

Part of the challenge of letting the business "drive" is providing enough quality information about the ongoing software development effort back into the business in order to support good business decision making. That's where transparency becomes crucial. The architect, in conjunction with development management, must create and nurture the means for regular, ongoing information feedback loops. This can be accomplished by a variety of lean software development techniques, such as big visible charts, continuous integration, and frequent releases of working software to the business starting early in the project.

Software development is fundamentally a design activity, in that it involves an ongoing process of decision making until the developed system goes into production. It is appropriate for software developers to make many decisions, but usually not to make business decisions. However, to the extent that the business community fails to fulfill its responsibility to provide direction, answer questions, and make business decisions for the software development team, it is actually delegating the business decision making to software developers. The architect must provide the macro-context for this ongoing series of micro-decisions made by developers, by communicating and protecting the software architecture and business objectives, and must seek to ensure that developers do not make business decisions. Technical decision making untethered to the commitments, expectations, and realities of the business—as articulated by the business community on an ongoing basis—amounts to costly speculation and often results in an unjustifiable expenditure of scarce resources.

The long-term interests of the software development team are best served when business drives.

Dave Muirhead is a veteran software craftsman and business technologist, and is an owner and principal consultant of Blue River Systems Group, LLC (BRSG), a Denver-based lean software development and technology strategy consulting firm.

Simplicity Before Generality, Use Before Reuse

Kevlin Henney

A COMMON PROBLEM IN COMPONENT FRAMEWORKS, class libraries, foundation services, and other infrastructure code is that many are designed to be general purpose without reference to concrete applications. This leads to a dizzying array of options and possibilities that are often unused, misused, or just not useful. Most developers work on specific systems: the quest for unbounded generality rarely serves them well (if at all). The best route to generality is through understanding known, specific examples and focusing on their essence to find an essential common solution. Simplicity through experience rather than generality through guesswork.

Favoring simplicity before generality acts as a tiebreaker between otherwise equally viable design alternatives. When there are two possible solutions, favor the one that is simpler and based on concrete need rather than the more intricate one that boasts of generality. Of course, it is entirely possible (and more than a little likely) that the simpler solution will turn out to be the more general one in practice. And if that doesn't turn out to be the case, it will be easier to change the simpler solution to what you now know you need than to change the "general" one that turns out not to be quite general enough in the right way.

Although well meant, many things that are designed just to be general purpose often end up satisfying no purpose. Software components should, first and foremost, be designed for use and to fulfill that use well. Effective generality comes from understanding, and understanding leads to simplification.

Generalization can allow us to reduce a problem to something more essential, resulting in an approach that embodies regularity across known examples, a regularity that is crisp, concise, and well grounded. However, too often generalization becomes a work item in itself, pulling in the opposite direction, adding to the complexity rather than reducing it. The pursuit of speculative generality often leads to solutions that are not anchored in the reality of actual development. They are based on assumptions that later turn out to be wrong, offer choices that later turn out not to be useful, and accumulate baggage that becomes difficult or impossible to remove, thereby adding to the accidental complexity developers and future architects must face.

Although many architects value generality, it should not be unconditional. People do not on the whole pay for (or need) generality: they tend to have a specific situation, and it is a solution to that specific situation that has value. We can find generality and flexibility in trying to deliver specific solutions, but if we weigh anchor and forget the specifics too soon, we end up adrift in a sea of nebulous possibilities, a world of tricky configuration options, overburdened (not just overloaded) parameter lists, long-winded interfaces, and not-quite-right abstractions. In pursuit of arbitrary flexibility, you can often lose valuable properties—accidental or intended—of alternative, simpler designs.

Kevlin Henney is an independent consultant and trainer. His work focuses on patterns and architecture, programming techniques and languages, and development process and practice. He is coauthor of A Pattern Language for Distributed Computing *and* On Patterns and Pattern Languages *(both from Wiley).*

Architects Must
Be Hands On

John Davies

A GOOD ARCHITECT SHOULD LEAD BY EXAMPLE. He (or she) should be able to fulfill any of the positions within his team, from wiring the network and configuring the build process to writing the unit tests and running benchmarks. Without a good understanding of the full range of technology, an architect is little more than a project manager. It is perfectly acceptable for team members to have more in-depth knowledge in their specific areas but it's difficult to imagine how team members can have confidence in their architect if the architect doesn't understand the technology. As has been said elsewhere, the architect is the interface between the business and the technology team, and thus must understand every aspect of the technology to be able to represent the team to the business without having to constantly refer others. Similarly the architect must understand the business in order to drive the team toward its goal of serving the business.

An architect is like an airline pilot: he might not look busy all of the time, but he uses decades of experience to constantly monitor the situation, taking immediate action if he sees or hears something out of the ordinary. The project manager (co-pilot) performs the day-to-day management, leaving the architect free from the hassles of mundane tasks and people management. Ultimately the architect should be responsible for the quality of the projects and their delivery to the business. This is difficult to achieve without authority, which is critical to the success of any project.

People learn best by watching others; it's how we learn as children. A good architect should be able to spot a problem, call the team together, and without picking out a victim, explain what the problem is or might be and provide an elegant workaround or solution. It is perfectly respectable for an architect to ask for help from the team. The team should feel it is part of the solution, but the architect should chair the discussion and identify the right solution(s).

Architects should be brought into the team at the earliest part of the project; they should not sit in an ivory tower dictating the way forward, but should be on the ground working with the team. Questions about direction or technology choices should not be spun off into separate investigations or new projects, but be made pragmatically through hands-on investigation or using advice from architect peers—all good architects are well connected.

Good architects should be experts in at least one tool of their trade, e.g., an IDE; remember they are hands on. It stands to reason that a software architect should know the IDE, a database architect should know the ER tool, and an information architect should know an XML modelling tool. A technical or enterprise architect, however, should be at least effective with all levels of tooling, from being able to monitor network traffic with Wireshark to modelling a complex financial message in XMLSpy—no level is too low or too high.

An architect usually comes with a good resume and impressive past. He can usually impress the business and technologists, but unless he can demonstrate his ability to be hands on, it's difficult to gain the respect of the team, difficult for the team to learn, and almost impossible for team members to deliver what they were originally employed to do.

John Davies is currently chief architect at Revolution Money in the U.S. He recently started a new company called Incept5.

Continuously Integrate

David Bartlett

THE BUILD AS A "BIG BANG" EVENT in project development is dead. The architect, whether an application or enterprise architect, should promote and encourage the use of continuous integration methods and tools for every project.

The term *continuous integration* (CI) was first coined by Martin Fowler in a design pattern. CI refers to a set practices and tools that ensure automatic builds and testing of an application at frequent intervals, usually on an integration server specifically configured for these tasks. The convergence of unit testing practices and tools in conjunction with automated build tools makes CI a must for any software project today.

Continuous integration targets a universal characteristic of the software development process: the integration point between source code and running application. At this integration point the many pieces of the development effort come together and are tested. You have probably heard the phrase "build early and often," which was a risk-reduction technique to ensure there were no surprises at this point in development. "Build early and often" has now been replaced by CI, which includes the build but also adds features that improve communication and coordination within the development team.

The most prominent part of a CI implementation is the build, which is usually automated. You have the ability to do a manual build, but builds can also be kicked off nightly or can be triggered by source code changes. Once the build is started, the latest version of the source code is pulled from the repository, and the CI tools attempts to build the project and then test it. Lastly, notification is sent out, detailing the results of the build process. These notifications can be sent in various forms including email or instant messages.

Continuous integration will provide a more stable and directed development effort. As an architect you will love it, but more important, your organization and your development teams will be more effective and efficient.

Dave Bartlett is an enthusiastic software professional with more than 25 years' experience as a programmer, developer, architect, manager, consultant, and instructor. He currently works for clients through Commotion Technologies, Inc., a private consulting firm, and lectures at Penn State University's Graduate Engineering School in Great Valley, Pennsylvania. His main work efforts today are with the Federal Reserve Bank of Philadelphia, helping to design and build web, portal, and composite applications for use within the Federal Reserve System and the United States Treasury.

Avoid Scheduling Failures

Norman Carnovale

FAILED PROJECTS CAN HAPPEN FOR A MULTITUDE OF REASONS. One of the most common sources of failure is altering the project schedule in midstream without proper planning. This kind of failure is avoidable, but it can require major effort on the part of multiple people. Adjusting the timeline or increasing resources on a project are not normally of concern. Problems start when you are asked to do more in the same timeline or when the schedule is shortened without reducing the workload.

The idea that schedules can be shortened in order to reduce cost or speed up delivery is a very common misconception. You'll commonly see attempts to require overtime or sacrifice "less important scheduled tasks" (like unit testing) as a way to reduce delivery dates, or increase functionality while keeping the delivery dates as is. Avoid this scenario at all costs. Remind those requesting the changes of the following facts:

- A rushed design schedule leads to poor design, bad documentation, and probable quality assurance or user acceptance problems.

- A rushed coding or delivery schedule has a direct relationship to the number of bugs delivered to the users.

- A rushed test schedule leads to poorly tested code and has a direct relationship to the number of testing issues encountered.

- All of the above lead to production issues, which are much more expensive to fix.

The end result is an increase in cost as opposed to a reduction. This is normally why the failures happen.

As an architect you will one day find yourself in the position of having to act quickly to increase the likelihood of success. Speak up early. First try to maintain quality by negotiating the originally planned timeline. If a shortened schedule is necessary, then try to move noncritical functionality to future release(s). Obviously this will take good preparation, negotiating skills, and a knack for influencing people. Prepare by sharpening your skills in those areas today. You will be glad you did.

Norman Carnovale is an IT architect working for Lockheed Martin Professional Services on Homeland Security–related projects. He was formerly a software consultant, instructor, and architect for Davalen, LLC (http://www.davalen.com), a Premier IBM Business Partner specializing in WebSphere Portlet Factory, WebSphere Portal, and Lotus Domino projects.

Architectural Tureoffs

Architectural Tradeoffs

Mark Richards

EVERY SOFTWARE ARCHITECT should know and understand that you can't have it all. It is virtually impossible to design an architecture that has high performance, high availability, a high level of security, and a high degree of abstraction all at the same time. There is a true story that software architects should know, understand, and be able to communicate to clients and colleagues. It is the story of a ship called the *Vasa*.

In the 1620s Sweden and Poland were at war. Wanting a quick end to this costly war, the king of Sweden commissioned the building of a ship called the *Vasa*. Now, this was no ordinary ship. The requirements for this ship were unlike any other ship of that time; it was to be more than 200 feet long, carry 64 guns on two gun decks, and have the ability to transport 300 troops safely across the waters into Poland. Time was of the essence, and money was tight (sound familiar?). The ship architect had never designed such a ship before. Smaller, single-gun deck ships were his area of expertise. Nevertheless, the ship's architect extrapolated on his prior experience and set out designing and building the *Vasa*. The ship was eventually built to specifications, and when the eventful day came for the launch, the ship proudly sailed into the harbor, fired its gun salute, and promptly sank to the bottom of the ocean.

The problem with the *Vasa* was obvious; anyone who has ever seen the deck of a large fighting ship from the 1600s and 1700s knows that the decks on those ships were crowded and unsafe, particularly in battle. Building a ship that was both a fighting ship and a transport ship was a costly mistake. The ship's architect, in an attempt to fulfill all of the king's wishes, created an unbalanced and unstable ship.

Software architects can learn a lot from this story and apply this unfortunate event to the design of software architecture. Trying to fulfill each and every requirement (as with the *Vasa*) creates an unstable architecture that essentially accomplishes nothing well. A good example of a tradeoff is the requirement to make a service-oriented architecture (SOA) perform as well as a point-to-point solution. Doing so usually requires you to bypass the various levels of abstraction created by an SOA approach, thereby creating an architecture that looks something like what you would typically order at your local Italian restaurant. There are several tools available to architects to determine what the tradeoffs should be when designing an architecture. Two popular methods are the Architecture Tradeoff Analysis Method (ATAM) and the Cost Benefit Analysis Method (CBAM). You can learn more about ATAM and CBAM by visiting the Software Engineering Institute (SEI) websites at *http://www.sei.cmu.edu/architecture/ata_method.html* and *http://www.sei.cmu.edu/architecture/cbam.html*, respectively.

Author bio available on page 9.

Database As a Fortress

Dan Chak

THE DATABASE IS WHERE ALL OF THE DATA, both input by your employees and collected from your customers, resides. User interfaces, business and application logic, and even employees will come and go, but your data lasts forever. Consequently, enough cannot be said about the importance of building a solid data model from Day One.

The exuberance over agile techniques has left many thinking that it's fine, or even preferable, to design applications as you go. Gone are the days of writing complex, comprehensive technical designs up front! The new school says deploy early and often. A line of code in production is better than 10 in your head. It seems almost too good to be true, and where your data is concerned, it is.

While business rules and user interfaces do evolve rapidly, the structures and relationships within the data you collect often do not. Therefore, it is critical to have your data model defined right from the start, both structurally and analytically. Migrating data from one schema to another in situ is difficult at best, time consuming always, and error prone often. While you can suffer bugs temporarily at the application layer, bugs in the database can be disastrous. Finding and fixing a data-layer design problem does not restore your data once it has been corrupted.

A solid data model is one that guarantees security of today's data, but is also extensible for tomorrow's. Guaranteeing security means being impervious to bugs that will—despite your best efforts—be pervasive in an ever-changing application layer. It means enforcing referential integrity. It means building in domain constraints wherever they are known. It means choosing appropriate keys that help you ensure your data's referential integrity and constraint satisfaction. Being extensible for tomorrow means properly normalizing your data so that you can easily add architectural layers upon your data model later. It means not taking shortcuts.

The database is the final gatekeeper of your precious data. The application layer, which is by design ephemeral, cannot be its own watchdog. For the database to keep proper guard, the data model must be designed to reject data that does not belong, and to prevent relationships that do not make sense. Keys, foreign key relationships, and domain constraints, when described in a schema, are succinct, easy to understand and verify, and ultimately self-documenting. Domain rules encoded in the data model are also physical and persistent; a change to application logic does not wash them away.

To get the most out of a relational database—to make it a true part of the application as opposed to simply a storehouse for application data—you need to have a solid understanding of what you are building from the start. As your product evolves, so too will the data layer, but at each phase of its evolution, it should always maintain its status as Fortress. If you trust it and bestow upon it the heavy responsibility of trapping bugs from other layers of your application, you will never be disappointed.

Dan Chak is the director of software development at CourseAdvisor Inc., a Washington Post company. He is the author of Enterprise Rails *(O'Reilly).*

Use Uncertainty
As a Driver

Kevlin Henney

CONFRONTED WITH TWO OPTIONS, most people think that the most important thing to do is to make a choice between them. In design (software or otherwise), it is not. The presence of two options is an indicator that you need to consider uncertainty in the design. Use the uncertainty as a driver to determine where you can defer commitment to details and where you can partition and abstract to reduce the significance of design decisions. If you hardwire the first thing that comes to mind, you're more likely to be stuck with it, so that incidental decisions become significant and the softness of the software is reduced.

One of the simplest and most constructive definitions of architecture comes from Grady Booch: "All architecture is design but not all design is architecture. Architecture represents the significant design decisions that shape a system, where significant is measured by cost of change." What follows from this is that an effective architecture is one that generally reduces the significance of design decisions. An ineffective architecture will amplify significance.

When a design decision can reasonably go one of two ways, an architect needs to take a step back. Instead of trying to decide between options A and B, the question becomes "How do I design so that the choice between A and B is less significant?" The most interesting thing is not actually the choice between A and B, but the fact that there is a choice between A and B (and that the appropriate choice is not necessarily obvious or stable).

An architect may need to go in circles before becoming dizzy and recognizing the dichotomy. Standing at a whiteboard (energetically) debating options with a colleague? Umming and ahhing in front of some code, deadlocked over whether to try one implementation or another? When a new requirement or a clarification of a requirement has cast doubt on the wisdom of a current implementation, that's uncertainty. Respond by figuring out what separation or encapsulation would isolate that decision from the code that ultimately depends on it. Without this sensibility the alternative response is often rambling code that, like a nervous interviewee, babbles away trying to compensate for uncertainty with a multitude of speculative and general options. Or, where a response is made with arbitrary but unjustified confidence, a wrong turn is taken at speed and without looking back.

There is often pressure to make a decision for the decision's sake. This is where options thinking can help. Where there is uncertainty over different paths a system's development might take, make the decision not to make a decision. Defer the actual decision until a decision can be made more responsibly, based on actual knowledge, but not so late that it is not possible to take advantage of that knowledge.

Architecture and process are interwoven, which is a key reason that architects should favor development lifecycles and architectural approaches that are empirical and elicit feedback, using uncertainty constructively to divide up both the system and the schedule.

Author bio available on page 37.

Warning: Problems in Mirror May Be Larger Than They Appear

Dave Quick

I'VE WORKED ON HUNDREDS OF SOFTWARE PROJECTS. Every one had issues that caused more problems than the team expected. Often, a small part of the team identified the issue early on and the majority dismissed or ignored it because they didn't understand how important it really was until it was too late.

The forces at work include:

- Issues that seemed trivial early in the project become critical after it is too late to fix them. While the boiling frog experiment may be folklore, it's a useful analogy for what happens in many projects.

- Individuals often face resistance when the rest of the team does not share their experience or knowledge. Overcoming this resistance requires unusual courage, confidence, and persuasiveness. It rarely happens, even with highly paid, experienced consultants specifically hired to help avoid such problems.

- Most software developers are optimists. Painful experience teaches us to temper our optimism, but without specific experience we tend toward optimism. Natural pessimists on development teams are often unpopular, even if they are consistently right. Few people will risk this reputation and take a stand against the majority without a very solid case. Most of us have had the "This makes me uncomfortable, but I can't explain why" feeling, but sharing it rarely wins any arguments.

- Every team member has a different view of what is more or less important. Their concerns are often focused on their personal responsibilities, not the project's goals.

- We all have blind spots, shortcomings that are difficult for us to recognize or to accept.

Some possible strategies to counteract these forces could include:

- Establish an organized approach to managing risks. One simple approach is to track risks the same way you track bugs. Anyone can identify a risk, and each risk is tracked until it is no longer a risk. Risks are prioritized and reviewed when their status changes or when there is new information. This helps remove emotion from the discussion and makes it easier to remember to re-evaluate risks periodically.

- When going against the majority, look for ways to help the rest of the team understand more easily. Encourage any team you're on to recognize the value in dissenting opinions and look for neutral ways to discuss them.

- "Bad smells" are worth recognizing. If the facts aren't there yet, look for the simplest tests that would provide the facts.

- Constantly test your understanding against the team and the customer. Tools such as a prioritized list of user stories can help, but are no substitute for regular communications with the customer and an open mind.

- Blind spots are, by definition, hard to recognize. People you trust to tell you the hard truth when you need it are a precious resource.

Dave Quick is the owner, chief architect, janitor, and sole employee of Thoughtful Arts. Thoughtful Arts develops off-the-shelf software for musicians and provides software design consulting for companies who develop music, or arts-oriented software.

Reuse Is About People and Education, Not Just Architecture

Jeremy Meyer

YOU MIGHT ADOPT THE APPROACH that a framework that is well designed, or an architecture that is carefully considered and cleverly implemented, will lend itself to reuse within your organization. The truth is that even the most beautiful, elegant, and reusable architecture, framework, or system will only be reused by people who:

Know It's There

Within your organization, developers or designers need to know that a design, framework, library, or fragment of code exists, and where they can find all the critical information about these elements (e.g., documentation, versions, and compatibility) in order to reuse them. It is a simple, logical truth that people won't look for things that they don't believe exist. You are more likely to succeed with reusable elements if the information about them is "pushed."

There are any number of methods for pushing information about reusable elements in an organization. These range from wiki pages with an RSS feed providing update information, useful in very large teams, to email announcing version updates in the source repository. In a tiny team, the designer or lead developer can inform his colleagues in personal conversations or by shouting it across the office. Ultimately, whatever your process for communicating about reusable elements, make sure you have one—don't leave it up to chance.

Know How to Use It

Understanding how to reuse an element depends on skills and training. Of course there are those people who (to use Donald Knuth's terminology) "resonate" with coding and design. We have all worked with them, the gifted developers and architects whose speed and depth of understanding is impressive, even scary. But these people are rare. The rest of your team might be made up of good, solid, intelligent developers and designers. They need to be taught.

Developers and designers might not know of the particular design pattern used in a design, or fully understand the inheritance model that the framework designer intended them to use. They need to be given easy access to that information in the form of up-to-date documentation, or even better, training. A little training goes a long way toward ensuring that everyone is on the same page when it comes to reuse.

Are Convinced That It's Better Than Doing It Themselves

People, and particularly developers, tend to prefer to solve problems themselves rather than ask for help. Asking how something works is a sign of weakness, or even an indication of ignorance. This has a lot to do with the maturity and personality type of your individual team members; "better than doing it themselves" means different things to different people. The "young guns" on your team will always want to write things themselves because it appeases their egos, whereas your more experienced people are more likely to accept that someone else has given thought to the problem domain and has something to offer in terms of a solution.

If your team doesn't know where to find reusable artifacts or how to reuse them, they will default to the natural, human position: they will build it themselves. And you will pay for it.

Jeremy Meyer has been designing and developing software for nearly 20 years, as well as teaching its mastery. He is currently a principal consultant for Borland Software in its modeling and design space.

There Is No 'I' in Architecture

Dave Quick

I KNOW, THERE REALLY IS AN 'I' IN ARCHITECTURE. But it's not a capital 'I', calling attention to itself, dominating discussion. The lowercase character fits neatly within the word. It's there only because it fulfills requirements for proper spelling and pronunciation.

How does that relate to us as software architects? Our egos can be our own worst enemy. Who hasn't experienced architects who:

- think they understand the requirements better than the customers,

- view developers as resources hired to implement their ideas, or

- get defensive when their ideas are challenged or ignore the ideas of others?

I suspect any experienced architect has fallen into at least one of these traps at some point. I've fallen into all of them and learned painful lessons from my mistakes.

Why does this happen?

- *We've had success.* Success and experience build self-confidence and allow us to become architects. Success leads to bigger projects. There is a fine line between self-confidence and arrogance. At some point the project is bigger than our personal ability. Arrogance sneaks in when we cross that line but don't know it yet.

- *People respect us.* Tough design questions provide a critical safety net. Our own defensiveness, arrogance, or emphasis on our experience can result in missed design questions.

- *We're human.* Architects pour themselves into each design. Criticism of your creation feels like criticism of you. Defensiveness is easy. Learning to stop it is hard. Pride in our accomplishments is easy. Recognizing our limitations without conscious effort is hard.

How do we avoid it?

- *Requirements don't lie.* With correct, complete requirements, any architecture that meets them is a good one. Work closely with the customer to make sure you both understand the business value each requirement provides. You don't drive the architecture, the requirements do. You do your best to serve their needs.

- *Focus on the team.* These are not just resources; they are your design collaborators and your safety net. People who feel unappreciated usually make a poor safety net. It's the teams' architecture, not yours alone. You provide guidance but everyone does the heavy lifting together. You need their help as much or more than they need yours.

- *Check your work.* The model is not the architecture. It is only your understanding of how the architecture should work. Work with your team to identify tests that demonstrate how the project's architecture supports each requirement.

- *Watch yourself.* Most of us fight our natural tendencies to defend our work, focus on our selfish interests, and see ourselves as the smartest person in the room. Pressure pushes these tendencies to the surface. Consider your interactions for a few minutes every day. Did you give everyone's ideas the respect and acknowledgment they deserved? Did you react negatively to well-meaning input? Do you really understand why someone disagreed with your approach?

Removing the 'I' from architecture doesn't guarantee success. It just removes a common source of failure that's entirely your fault.

Author bio available on page 51.

Get the 1,000-Foot View

Erik Doernenburg

AS ARCHITECTS, WE WANT TO KNOW how good the software is that we are developing. Its quality has an obvious external aspect—the software should be of value to its users—but there is also a more elusive internal aspect to quality, having to do with the clarity of the design, the ease with which we can understand, maintain, and extend the software. When pressed for a definition, this is where we usually end up saying "I know it when I see it." But how can we see quality?

In an architecture diagram, little boxes represent entire systems and lines between them can mean anything: a dependency, the flow of data, or a shared resource such as a bus. These diagrams are a 30,000-foot view, like a landscape seen from a plane. Typically the only other view available is the source code, which is comparable to a ground-level view. Both views fail to convey much information about the quality of the software: one is too high level and the other provides so much information that we cannot see structure. Clearly, what is missing is a view in between—a 1,000-foot view.

This 1,000-foot view would provide information at the right level. It aggregates large amounts of data and multiple metrics, such as method count, class fan out, or cyclomatic complexity. The actual view very much depends on a specific aspect of quality. It can be a visual representation of a dependency graph, a bar chart that shows metrics at a class level, or a sophisticated polymetric view that correlates multiple input values.

Manually creating such views and keeping them in sync with the software is a hopeless endeavor. We need tools that create these views from the only true source, the source code. For some views—a design structure matrix, for example—commercial tools exist, but it is also surprisingly easy to create specialized views by combining small tools that extract data and metrics with generic visualization packages. A simple example would be to load the output from checkstyle, which is essentially a set of metrics on the class and method level, into a spreadsheet to render charts. The same metrics could also be shown as a tree-map using the InfoViz toolkit. A great tool to render complex dependency graphs is GraphViz.

Once a suitable view is available, software quality becomes a little less subjective. It is possible to compare the software under development with a handful of similar systems. Comparing different revisions of the same system will give an indication of trends, while comparing views of different subsystems can highlight outliers. Even with just a single diagram, we can rely on our ability to spot patterns and perceive aesthetics. A well-balanced tree probably represents a successful class hierarchy; a harmonious set of boxes might show code that is organized into appropriately sized classes. Most of the time a very simple relationship holds: if it looks good, it probably is good.

Erik Doernenburg is a technology principal at ThoughtWorks, Inc., where he helps clients with the design and implementation of large-scale enterprise solutions.

Try Before Choosing

Erik Doernenburg

CREATING AN APPLICATION REQUIRES MAKING MANY DECISIONS. Some might involve choosing a framework or library, while others revolve around the use of specific design patterns. In either case the responsibility for the decision generally lies with the architect on the team. A stereotypical architect might gather all the information that can be gathered, then mull over it for a while, and finally decree the solution from the ivory tower for it to be implemented by the developers. Not surprisingly, there is a better way.

In their work on lean development, Mary and Tom Poppendieck describe a technique for making decisions. They argue that we should delay commitment until the last responsible moment; that is, the moment at which, if the team does not make a decision, it is made for them—when inaction results in an outcome that is not (easily) reversible. This is prudent because the later a decision is made, the more information is available on which to base the decision. However, in many cases more information is not the same as enough information, and we also know that the best decisions are made in hindsight. What does this mean for the good architect?

The architect should constantly be on the lookout for decisions that will have to be made soon. Provided the team has more than a handful of developers and practices collective code ownership, the architect can, when such a decision point approaches, ask several developers to come up with a solution to the problem and go with it for a while. As the last responsible moment approaches, the team meets to assess the benefits and drawbacks of the different solutions.

Usually, now with the benefit of hindsight, the best solution to the problem is apparent to everybody. The architect does not have to make the decision, he or she merely orchestrates the decision-making process.

This approach works for small decisions as well as for large ones. It can allow a team to figure out whether or not to use the Hibernate templates provided by the Spring framework, but it can equally answer the question of which JavaScript framework to use. The duration for which the different approaches evolve is obviously very dependent on the complexity of the decision.

Trying two or even more approaches to the same problem requires more effort than making a decision upfront and then just implementing one. However, chances are that an upfront decision leads to a solution that is later recognized to be suboptimal, leaving the architect with a dilemma: either the team rolls back the current implementation or it lives with the consequences, both of which result in wasted effort. Even worse, it is entirely possible that nobody on the team recognizes that the approach chosen is not the best one, because none of the alternatives was explored. In this case, effort is wasted without any chance of addressing the waste. After all, trying multiple approaches might be the least expensive option.

Author bio available on page 57.

Understand the
Business Domain

Mark Richards

EFFECTIVE SOFTWARE ARCHITECTS understand not only technology but also the business domain of a problem space. Without business domain knowledge, it is difficult to understand the business problem, goals, and requirements, and therefore difficult to design an effective architecture to meet the requirements of the business.

It is the role of the software architect to understand the business problem, business goals, and business requirements and translate those requirements into a technical architecture solution capable of meeting them. Knowing the business domain helps an architect decide which patterns to apply, how to plan for future extensibility, and how to prepare for ongoing industry trends. For example, some business domains (e.g., insurance) lend themselves well to a service-oriented architecture approach where as other business domains (e.g., financial markets) lend themselves more toward a workflow-based architecture approach. Knowing the domain helps you decide which architecture pattern may work best to satisfy the specific needs of the organization.

Knowing the industry trends of a specific domain can also help a software architect in designing an effective architecture. For example, in the insurance domain, there is an increasing trend toward "on-demand" auto insurance, where you only pay for auto insurance when you actually drive your car. This type of insurance is great if you park your car at the airport on Monday morning, fly off to your work destination, and return Friday to drive back home.

Understanding such industry trends enables you as a software architect to plan for these trends in the architecture, even if the company you are working with hasn't planned for them yet as part of its business model.

Understanding the specific goals of the business also helps you design an effective architecture. For example, do the goals of the particular business you are working for include non-organic growth through heavy mergers and acquisitions? The answer to this question may influence the type of architecture you design. If the answer is yes, the architecture might include many layers of abstraction to facilitate the merging of business components. If the goals of the business include increased market share through a heavy online presence, then high availability is most likely going to be a very important attribute. As a software architect, always understand the goals of the company you are working with, and validate that the architecture can support these goals.

The most successful architects I know are those who have broad hands-on technical knowledge coupled with a strong knowledge of a particular domain. These software architects are able to communicate with C-level executives and business users using the domain language that these folks know and understand. This in turn creates a strong level of confidence that the software architect knows what he or she is doing. Knowing the business domain allows a software architect to better understand the problems, issues, goals, data, and processes, all of which are key factors when designing an effective enterprise architecture.

Author bio available on page 11.

Programming Is
an Act of Design

Einar Landre

KRISTEN NYGAARD, FATHER OF OBJECT-ORIENTED PROGRAMMING and the Simula programming language, used to say *programming is learning*. Accepting the fact that programming—or more precisely, software development—is a processes of discovery and learning, not a process of engineering and construction, is fundamental to bringing software practices forward. Applying the concepts of traditional engineering and construction on software development does not work. The problems have been documented and commented upon by leading software thinkers for more than 30 years. As an example, in 1987 Fredric Brooks, Jr., stated in the "Report of the Defense Science Board Task Force on Military Software" that the document-driven, specify-then-build approach lies at the heart of many software problems.

So where should the software industry look to improve its practices? What about the industries involved in production of sophisticated mass-market products such as cars, pharmaceutical drugs, or semiconductors?

Let's take a look at the car industry. When planning a new model, the first thing is to choose a concept or archetype. It's primarily an architectural positioning mechanism. The BMW X6 is an example of a new concept that combines the properties of an SUV and a coupe into what BMW calls a *sports activity coupe*. Before you can purchase a new X6, BMW has invested thousands of hours and millions of dollars in both its vehicle and manufacturing design. When BMW receives your order, one of its assembly lines will kick in and produce your customized version of the X6.

So what can we learn from this car-maker scenario? The important lesson is that the making of a new car involves two processes: the first process is the creative design process, including establishing the required assembly lines. The second process is the manufacturing of cars in line with customer specifications. In many ways these are the processes we find in the software industry as well. The challenge is what we put into the terms.

In the article "What is software design?", Jack Reeves suggests that the only artifact of software engineering that satisfies the criteria for a design document, as such a document is understood and used in classical engineering, is the source code. The manufacturing of the software is automated and taken care of by the compiler, build, and test scripts.

By accepting that carving out source code is an act of design, not an act of construction, we are in a position to adopt useful management practices that are proven to work. Those are the practices used to manage creative and unpredictable work such as developing a new car, a new medical drug, or a new computer game. We talk about the practices of agile product management and lean production such as SCRUM. These practices focus on maximizing return on investment in terms of customer value.

For the software industry to capitalize on these practices, we must remember this: programming is an act of design, not an act of construction.

Author bio available on page 13.

Give Developers Autonomy

Philip Nelson

MOST ARCHITECTS BEGIN THEIR CAREERS AS DEVELOPERS. An architect has new responsibilities and greater authority in determining how a system is built. You may find it difficult to let go of what you did as a developer in your new role as an architect. Worse, you may feel it's important for you to exercise a lot of control over how developers do their work to implement the design. It will be very important to your success and your team's success to give all of your teammates enough autonomy to exercise their own creativity and abilities.

As a developer you rarely get the time to sit back and really look at how the whole system fits together. As an architect, this is your main focus. While developers are furiously building classes, methods, tests, user interfaces, and databases, you should be making sure that all those pieces work well together. Listen for points of pain and try to improve them. Are people having trouble writing tests? Improve the interfaces and limit dependencies. Do you understand where you actually need abstraction and where you don't? Work for domain clarity. Do you know what order to build things in? Build your project plan. Are developers consistently making common mistakes using an API you designed? Make the design more obvious. Do people really understand the design? Communicate and make it clear. Do you really understand where you need to scale and where you don't? Work with your customers and learn their business model.

If you're doing a great job of being an architect, you really shouldn't have enough time to interfere with developers. You do need to watch closely enough to see that the design is being implemented as intended. You do not need to be standing over people's shoulders to accomplish that goal. It's reasonable to make suggestions when you see people struggling, but it's even better if you create the environment where they come and ask you for suggestions. If you are good, you will deftly walk the fine line between guaranteeing a successful architecture and limiting the creative and intellectual life of your developers and teammates.

Philip Nelson is a technology generalist whose career began in hardware; moved to networks, systems, and administration; and finally changed to software development and architecture, where he found the most interesting things were going on. He has worked on software problems in transportation, finance, manufacturing, marketing, and many infrastructure-related areas.

Time Changes Everything

Philip Nelson

ONE OF THE THINGS I've been most entertained by as the years have gone by is observing what things have lasted and what haven't. So many patterns, frameworks, paradigm changes, and algorithms—all argued for with passion by smart people, thinking of the long term, balancing all the known issues—have not warranted more than a yawn over the long haul. Why? What is history trying to tell us?

Pick a Worthy Challenge

This one is tricky for a software architect. Challenges or problems are given to us, so we don't have the luxury of choosing, right? It's not that simple. First of all, we often make the mistake of believing that we can't influence what we are asked to do. Usually we can, but it gets us out of our comfort zone in the technology space. There are dragons there when we don't choose to do the right things. Time passes, we have worked diligently and hard solving the requested challenge, and in the end it doesn't matter: we didn't do what was really needed and our work is wasted. Over time, a good solution to the right challenge will probably outlast all others.

Simple Rules

We say it to ourselves: keep it simple, stupid. We say it, but we don't do it. We don't do it because we don't have to. We are smart and we can handle some complexity and easily justify it because it adds agility to our design, because it is more elegant to our aesthetic sensibilities, because we believe we can anticipate the future. Then time passes; you walk away from the project for a year or more. When you come back to it, you almost always wonder why you did what you did. If you had to do it all over again, you would probably do it differently. Time does this to us. It makes us look silly. It is good to realize this early, get over yourself, and really try to learn what simple means in the lens that only time can grind.

Be Happy with That Old Stuff

Architects love to search for the "one true way": the methodology or school of thought that provides the predictability we crave and the clear answers that always seem just out of reach. The problem is that whatever guiding light you have in one year will probably not match the guiding light you have in a couple of years, much less a decade later. As you look back, you will always be looking at designs that don't match your current expectations. Learn to embrace that old stuff, and resist the temptation to think you should go back and "fix" it. Was the solution an appropriate one for the problem? Did it solve the needs of the problem? Keep these as your measure—you will be a lot happier.

Author bio available on page 65.

"Software Architect" Has Only Lowercase *a*'s; Deal with It

Barry Hawkins

A DISAPPOINTING TREND has been in bloom for some time now within software development: the attempt to professionalize the practice of software architecture as one on par with the classical school of Architecture. This seems to stem from some need to further legitimize one's accomplishment beyond acknowledgment among one's peers and employer. By comparison, Architecture itself was not professionalized until the late 19th century, at least a few millennia after the practice had been around. It would be no great stretch to say that some software architects seem a bit eager by comparison.

Software architecture is a craft, and it certainly takes practice and discipline to achieve success in the field. That said, software development is still a relatively nascent endeavor. We don't even know enough about this practice to adequately professionalize it. Despite its youth, software development's product has become a highly valued tool, and as such, the accomplished individuals (as well as those who wish to be seen as accomplished) have enjoyed levels of compensation on par with the leading professional fields, including medicine, accounting, and law.

Practitioners of software development enjoy considerable compensation for work that is highly creative and exploratory. The fruits of our labors have been used to accomplish many significant milestones, some that benefit all of mankind. The barriers to entry are largely one's own merit and opportunity; the fully professionalized fields undergo programs of study and internship that dwarf our own. Dwell on that for a moment and ponder how much cause we have to be content, and just how brash it is to insist that software architect be considered a title that sits as peer to Lawyer, Doctor, and Architect.

The title of software architect has only lowercase *a*'s; deal with it.

Barry Hawkins has played various roles in his 13 years in the software industry, from lone developer to team lead to Agile coach and mentor. Barry is one of the few native Atlantans, currently specializing in coaching and mentoring for Agile software development and domain-driven design.

Scope Is the Enemy of Success

Dave Quick

SCOPE REFERS TO A PROJECT'S SIZE. How much time, effort, and resources? What functionality at what level of quality? How difficult to deliver? How much risk? What constraints exist? The answers define a project's scope. Software architects love the challenge of big, complicated projects. The potential rewards can even tempt people to artificially expand a project's scope to increase its apparent importance. Expanding scope is the enemy of success because the probability of failure grows faster than expected. Doubling a project's scope often increases its probability of failure by an order of magnitude.

Why does it work this way? Consider some examples:

- Intuition tells us to double our time or resources to do twice as much work. History[1] says impacts are not as linear as intuition suggests. For example, a four-person team will expend more than twice the communication effort as a team of two.

- Estimation is far from an exact science. Who hasn't seen features that were much harder to implement than expected?

Of course, some projects aren't worth doing without some built-in size and complexity. While a text editor without the ability to enter text might be easy to build, it wouldn't be a text editor. So, what strategies can help to reduce or manage scope in real-world projects?

- *Understand the real needs.* The capabilities a project must deliver are a set of requirements. Requirements define functionality or qualities of functionality. Question any requirements not explained in terms of measurable value to the customer. If it has no effect on the company's bottom line, why is it a requirement?

---

1 See *The Mythical Man-Month: Essays on Software Engineering,* by Frederick Brooks (Addison-Wesley Professional).

- *Divide and conquer.* Look for opportunities to divide up the work into smaller independent chunks. It is easier to manage several small independent projects than one large project with interdependent parts.

- *Prioritize.* The world of business changes rapidly. Large projects' requirements change many times before they're completed. Important requirements usually remain important as the business changes, while others change or even evaporate. Prioritization lets you deliver the most important requirements first.

- *Deliver results as soon as possible.* Few people know what they want before they have it. A famous cartoon shows the evolution of a project to build a child's swing based on what the customer said and what various roles in the project understood. The complicated result only faintly resembles a swing. The last panel, titled "What would have worked", shows a simple swing using an old tire. When the customer has something to try, the solution may be simpler than expected. Building the most important things first gets you the most important feedback early, when you need it most.

Agile advocates[2] exhort us to build "the simplest thing that could possibly work". Complex architectures fail far more often than simpler architectures. Reducing project scope often results in a simpler architecture, and is one of the most effective strategies an architect can apply to improve the odds of success.

Author bio available on page 51.

---

2 See *eXtreme Programming eXplained: Embrace Change*, by Kent Beck (Addison-Wesley Professional).

Value Stewardship Over Showmanship

Barry Hawkins

WHEN AN ARCHITECT ENTERS A PROJECT, there is an understandable desire to prove his or her worth. Being assigned the role of software architect typically indicates implicit trust on the part of the company in the architect's technical leadership, and it only follows that the architect would desire to make good on that expectation as soon as possible. Unfortunately, there are those who labor under the misapprehension that proving one's worth consists of showmanship—bedazzling if not baffling the team with one's technical brilliance.

Showmanship, the act of appealing to your audience, is important in marketing, but it's counterproductive to leading a software development project. Architects must win the respect of their team by providing solid leadership and by truly understanding the technical and business domain in which they are expected to operate.

Stewardship, taking responsibility and care of another's property, is the appropriate role of an architect. An architect must act in the best interests of his customer and not pander to the needs of his own ego.

Software architecture is about serving the needs of one's customers, typically through direction from those with domain expertise that surpasses one's own. Pursuing successful software development will lead one to create solutions of compromise, balancing the cost and complexity of implementation against the time and effort available to a project. That time and effort are the resources of the company, which the software architect must steward without self-serving undercurrents. Unduly complex systems that sport the latest hot framework or technology buzzword seldom do so without some sacrifice at the company's expense. Much like an investment broker, the architect is being allowed to play with his client's money, based on the premise that his activity will yield an acceptable return on investment.

Value stewardship over showmanship; never forget that you are playing with other people's money.

Author bio available on page 69.

Software Architecture Has Ethical Consequences

Michael Nygard

THE ETHICAL DIMENSION IN SOFTWARE is obvious when we are talking about civil rights, identity theft, or malicious software. But it arises in less exotic circumstances. If programs are successful, they affect the lives of thousands or millions of people. That impact can be positive or negative. The program can make their lives better or worse—even if just in minute proportions.

Every time I make a decision about how a program behaves, I am really deciding what my users can and cannot do, in ways more inflexible than law. There is no appeals court for required fields or mandatory workflow.

Another way to think about it is in terms of multipliers. Think back to the last major Internet worm, or when a big geek movie came out. No doubt, you heard or read a story about how much productivity this thing would cost the country. You can always find some analyst with an estimate of outrageous damages, blamed on anything that takes people away from their desks. The real moral of this story isn't about innumeracy in the press, or self-aggrandizing accountants. It's about multipliers, and the effect they can have.

Suppose you have a decision to make about a particular feature. You can do it the easy way in about a day, or the hard way in about a week. Which way should you do it? Suppose that the easy way makes four new fields required, whereas doing it the hard way makes the program smart enough to handle incomplete data. Which way should you do it?

Required fields seem innocuous, but they are always an imposition of your will on users. They force users to gather more information before starting their jobs. This often means they have to keep their data on Post-It notes until they've got everything together at the same time, resulting in lost data, delays, and general frustration.

As an analogy, suppose I'm putting up a sign on my building. Is it OK to mount the sign just six feet up on the wall, forcing pedestrians to duck or go around it? It's easier for me to hang the sign if I don't need a ladder and scaffold, and the sign wouldn't even block the sidewalk. I get to save an hour installing the sign, at the expense of taking two seconds away from every pedestrian passing my store. Over the long run, all of those two-second diversions are going to add up to many, many times more than the hour that I saved.

It's not ethical to worsen the lives of others, even a small bit, just to make things easy for yourself. Successful software affects millions of people. Every decision you make imposes your will on your users. Always be mindful of the impact your decisions have on those people. You should be willing to bear large burdens to ease theirs.

Author bio available on page 17.

Skyscrapers Aren't Scalable

Michael Nygard

WE OFTEN HEAR SOFTWARE ENGINEERING COMPARED to building sky-scrapers, dams, or roads. It's true in some important aspects.

The hardest part of civil engineering isn't designing a building that will stand up once it is finished, but figuring out the construction process. The construction process has to go from a bare site to a finished building. In the interim, every worker must be able to apply his trade, and the unfinished structure has to stand up the whole time. We can take a lesson from that when it comes to deploying large integrated systems. ("Integrated" includes virtually every enterprise and web application!) Traditional "big bang" deployments are like stacking up a pile of beams and girders, throwing them into the air, and expecting them to stick together in the shape of a building.

Instead, we should plan to deploy one component at a time. Whether this is a replacement or a greenfield project, this has two large benefits.

First, when we deploy software, we are exposing ourselves to the accumulated technical risk embodied in the code. By deploying one component at a time, we spread technical risk out over a longer period of time. Every component has its own chance to fail in production, letting us harden each one independently.

The second large benefit is that it forces us to create well-defined interfaces between components. Deploying a single component of a new system often means reverse-integrating it with the old system. Therefore, by the time deployment is complete, each component has worked with two different systems: the original and the replacement. Nothing is reusable until it has been reused, so piecewise deployment automatically means greater reusability. In practice, it also leads to better coherence and looser coupling.

Conversely, there are some important ways that civil engineering analogies mislead us. In particular, the concreteness of the real world pushes us toward a waterfall process. After all, nobody starts building a skyscraper without knowing where it's going or how tall it should be. Adding floors to an existing building is costly, disruptive, and risky, so we try to avoid it. Once designed, the skyscraper isn't supposed to change its location or height. Skyscrapers aren't scalable.

We cannot easily add lanes to roads, but we've learned how to easily add features to software. This isn't a defect of our software processes, but a virtue of the medium in which we work. It's OK to release an application that only does a few things, as long as users value those things enough to pay for them. In fact, the earlier you release your application, the greater the net present value of the whole thing will be.

"Early release" may appear to compete with "incremental deployment," but they can actually work together quite well. Early release of individual components means that each one can iterate independently. In fact, it will force you to work out thorny issues like continuous availability during deployments and protocol versioning.

It's rare to find a technique that simultaneously provides higher commercial value and better architectural qualities, but early deployment of individual components offers both.

Author bio available on page 17.

Heterogeneity
Wins

Edward Garson

THE NATURAL EVOLUTION OF COMPUTER TECHNOLOGY has brought about important changes to the tools that architects can use to build software systems. These changes have brought about a resurgence of interest in polyglot programming, which refers to the use of more than one core language in the provision of a software system.

Polyglot programming is not a new concept: one prominent example from the past is frontend Visual Basic clients supported by COM objects authored in C++ on the backend. Fundamentally speaking, this architecture leveraged what those languages were good at in their heyday.

So, what changes took place to fuel this renewed interest in polyglot programming?

The change is that technical standards, together with ever-increasing bandwidth and computing resources, conspired to make text-based protocols viable; gone are the days of arcane binary protocols as a prerequisite to efficient distributed systems. Text-based remote interoperability largely began with XML/SOAP-based web services and continues to evolve with RESTful architectural styles and other supporting (but no less important) protocols such as Atom and XMPP.

This new breed of technologies creates far broader opportunities for heterogeneous development than ever before, simply because the payload is formatted text, which is universally generated and consumed. Heterogeneous development affords using the right tool for the job, and text-based interop has blown the doors off what was previously possible.

Architects can now combine specific, powerful tools that move the yardstick from previously being able to employ the right language to now being able to employ the right paradigm. Programming languages support different paradigms, in that some are object-oriented, while others are functional or excel at concurrent programming. Some of these paradigms are a perfect match for particular problems or domains, while others are a poor fit. Today, however, it is possible to "mash up" some rather unconventional and seemingly dissonant tools into elegant solutions rather more easily than in the past.

The effect of this change has begun, and manifests itself as a combinatorial increase in the architectural topology of modern software systems. This is not just a reflection of their inherent diversity, but a testament to new possibilities.

While choice is not always a good thing, it is "less worse" than the alternative in the context of modern software architecture. As an industry, we are faced with very serious problems[1] and we need all the interoperability we can get, particularly as the incumbent platforms are not well equipped to resolve them.[2]

Your job as architect has become even more challenging because technology silos are crumbling in the face of new possibilities: embrace this, think outside the stack, and leverage the new diversity: heterogeneity wins.

Edward Garson has been passionate about technology since learning to program in Logo on the Apple II. He currently works as a software architect in the Center for Agile Practices at Zuhlke Engineering, a leading Swiss-based technology firm.

1 The impending multicore era may well prove to be the most significant problem yet faced by the software development community.
2 See "The Free Lunch is Over," by Herb Sutter (*http://www.gotw.ca/publications/concurrency-ddj.htm*).

It's All About Performance

Craig Russell

IMAGINE A PERSONAL VEHICLE THAT IS ROOMY, comfortable, fuel efficient, inexpensive to produce, and 98% recyclable. You want one? Sure. Everyone does. Just one problem: its top speed is 6 miles/hour (10 km/hour). Still want one? This small example demonstrates that performance is just as important as any other criterion.

The reason many designers put performance at the bottom of their lists might be that computers are so much faster at computation than their human counterparts that the designers assume that the speed of the system will be acceptable. And if today's systems aren't fast enough, Moore's Law will take care of everything. But hardware speed is only part of the system.

Performance is sometimes thought of as a simple measurement of the time it takes for a system to respond to user input. But system designers must consider many aspects of performance, including performance of the analysts and programmers who implement the design; performance of the human interactions of the system; and performance of the noninteractive components.

Performance of the people building the system is often called productivity, and it is important because it directly affects the cost and schedule of the project. A team that delivers a project late and over budget has a lot of 'splainin' to do. Using tools and prebuilt components can dramatically affect how quickly the system can be built and start returning value.

Performance of the human interactions is critical to acceptance of the system. Many factors of system design contribute to this aspect of performance, response time being perhaps the most obvious. But response time isn't the only factor. Just as important are intuitiveness of the interface and number of gestures required to achieve a goal, both of which directly affect performance.

More than response time per se, a good system specification will measure task time, defined as the time required to complete a domain-specific task, including all human interactions with the system. In addition to system response time, this measurement includes operator think time and operator data entry time, which are not under the control of the system. But including these times gives motivation to the proper design of the human interface. Proper attention to the way information is presented and the number of gestures required to complete the task will result in better human operational performance.

Performance of the noninteractive components is equally important to the success of the system. For example, a "nightly" batch run that takes more than 24 hours to complete will result in an unusable system. Performance of the disaster recovery component is also a critical consideration. In case of total destruction of one part of the system, how quickly can operational status be restored, in order to allow normal business to resume?

When considering the implementation and operation of a successful system, architects and designers should always pay careful attention to performance.

Craig Russell is a practicing software architect specializing in object persistence and distributed systems. He currently works as a senior staff engineer at Sun Microsystems.

Engineer in the White Spaces

Michael Nygard

A SYSTEM CONSISTS OF INTERDEPENDENT PROGRAMS. We call the arrangement of these programs and their relationships *architecture*. When we diagram these systems, we often represent individual programs or servers as simplistic little rectangles, connected by arrows.

One little arrow might mean, "Synchronous request/reply using SOAP-XML over HTTP." That's quite a lot of information for one glyph to carry. There's not usually enough room to write all that, so we label the arrow with either "XML over HTTP" from an internal perspective, or "SKU Lookup" for the external perspective.

That arrow bridging programs looks like a direct contact, but it isn't. The white space between the boxes is filled with hardware and software components. This substrate may contain:

- Network interface cards
- Network switches
- Firewalls
- IDS and IPS
- Message queues or brokers
- XML transformation engines
- FTP servers

- "Landing zone" tables
- Metro-area SoNET rings
- MPLS gateways
- Trunk lines
- Oceans
- Cable-finding fishing trawlers

There will always be four or five computers between program A and B, running their software for packet switching, traffic analysis, routing, threat analysis, and so on. As the architect bridging those programs, you must consider this substrate.

I saw one arrow labeled "Fulfillment". One server was inside my client's company, the other server was in a different one. That arrow, critical to customer satisfaction, unpacked a chain of events that resembled a game of "Mousetrap" more than a single interface. Messages went to message brokers that dumped to files, which were picked up by a periodic FTP job, and so on. That one "interface" had more than 20 steps.

It's essential to understand the static and dynamic loads that arrow must carry. Instead of just "SOAP-XML over HTTP," that one little arrow should also say, "Expect one query per HTTP request and send back one response per HTTP reply. Expect up to 100 requests per second, and deliver responses in less than 250 milliseconds 99.999% of the time."

There's more we need to know about that arrow:

- What if the caller hits it too often? Should the receiver drop requests on the floor, refuse politely, or make the best effort possible?

- What should the caller do when replies take more than 250 milliseconds? Should it retry the call? Should it wait until later, or assume the receiver has failed and move on without that function?

- What happens when the caller sends a request with version 1.0 of the protocol and gets back a reply in version 1.1? What if it gets back some HTML instead of XML? Or an MP3 file instead of XML?

- What happens when one end of the interface disappears for a while?

Answering these questions is the essence of engineering the white spaces.

Author bio available on page 17.

Talk the Talk

Mark Richards

IN ANY PROFESSION, jargon is used so that individuals within that profession can effectively communicate with one another. Lawyers talk to one another about habeas corpus, voir dire, and venire; carpenters talk to one another about butt joints, lap joints, and flux; and software architects talk to one another about ROA, Two Step View, and Layer Supertype. Wait, what was that?

It is imperative that software architects, regardless of the platform they are working in, have an effective means of communication among one another. One of those means of communication is through architecture and design patterns. To be an effective software architect you must understand the basic architecture and design patterns, recognize when those patterns are being used, know when to apply the patterns, and be able to communicate to other architects and developers using them.

Architecture and design patterns can be classified into four basic categories: enterprise architecture patterns, application architecture patterns, integration patterns, and design patterns. These categories are generally based on the level of scope within the overall architecture. Enterprise architecture patterns deal with the high-level architecture, whereas design patterns deal with how individual components within the architecture are structured and behave.

Enterprise architecture patterns define the framework for the high-level architecture. Some of the more common architecture patterns include event-driven architecture (EDA), service-oriented architecture (SOA), resource-oriented architecture (ROA), and pipeline architecture.

Application architecture patterns specify how applications or subsystems within the scope of a larger enterprise architecture should be designed. Some common pattern catalogs in this category include the well-known J2EE design patterns (e.g., Session Façade and Transfer Object) and the application architecture patterns described in Martin Fowler's book *Patterns of Enterprise Application Architecture* (Addison-Wesley Professional).

Integration patterns are important for designing and communicating concepts surrounding the sharing of information and functionality between components, applications, and subsystems. Some examples of integration patterns include file sharing, remote procedure calls, and numerous messaging patterns. You can find these patterns at *http://www.enterpriseintegrationpatterns.com/eaipatterns.html*.

Knowing the basic design patterns as described by the Gang of Four book *Design Patterns: Elements of Reusable Object-Oriented Software* (Addison-Wesley Professional) is a must for any software architect. Although these patterns may appear to be too low-level for a software architect, they are part of a standard vocabulary that makes for effective communication between architects and developers.

It is also important to be aware of and understand the various anti-patterns as well. *Anti-patterns*, a term coined by Andrew Koenig, are repeatable processes that produce ineffective results. Some of the more well-known anti-patterns include Analysis Paralysis, Design By Committee, Mushroom Management, and Death March. Knowing these patterns will help you avoid the many pitfalls you will most likely experience. You can find a list of the common anti-patterns at *http://en.wikipedia.org/wiki/Anti-patterns*.

Software architects need the ability to communicate with one another in a clear, concise, and effective way. The patterns are there; it is up to us as software architects to learn and understand these patterns so we can "walk the walk and talk the talk."

Author bio available on page 9.

Context Is King

Edward Garson

I FEEL THERE IS A CERTAIN IRONY in trying to impart something about architectural ideals, when the very premise I wish to begin with is that effectively there are no ideals. If this is indeed the case, then surely there is nothing to write; I am a contradiction and by doing this I run the risk of the universe imploding or something like that.

But alas, *ceci n'est pas une pipe.*

One of the most valuable lessons that I have learned as a software architect is that context is king, and simplicity its humble servant. What this means in practical terms is that context is the only force that trumps simplicity when you're making architectural decisions.

When I say *context*, I refer not only to high-level, immediate forces such as key business drivers, but also to elements in the periphery, such as emerging technologies and thought leadership on diverse topics. Indeed, good architects keep track of several fast-moving targets.

What constitutes good architecture? It is the product of decisions made within a context usually tainted with multiple competing priorities. Those competing priorities mean that sometimes the most important decisions are not about what you put in, but rather what you omit. The currency of good architecture is simply astute decision-making (while the products are all only about communicating your intent).

Historically, there have been some fascinating examples of the influence that context can have on architecture. A favorite example involves the database selected to support an ambitious new software system for a modern battlefield tank.[1] (Deciding what database to use is not usually architecturally significant; this example merely serves to illustrate a point.)

When it came time to choose the database, the team assessed many. It found that while the tank was moving quickly over undulating terrain while tracking a target, the majority of the databases were capable of supporting the maximal throughput required of the navigation and targeting systems. But the team was taken by surprise when it discovered that firing the main gun on the tank caused such a strong electromagnetic pulse that it totally crashed the onboard systems and of course the database along with it! On a modern battlefield, a tank without its software running is quite literally in the dark. In this context, recovery time was the overwhelming factor in the choice of database, and no database did that better at the time than InterBase,[2] and that is why it was chosen for the M1 Abrams tank.

So, while newsgroups rage with the flames of technology debates of X versus Y, it is idle amusement. The reason these debates rage is often not because of huge disparities in their technical merits, but rather because there are more subtle differences between them, and what features individuals value more than others when there is no guiding context to act as a trump card.

Your team should be free of ideals, reflect on context in the first instance, and reach for the simplest solutions from there.

Author bio available on page 79.

1 A tank, despite its extremely dubious purpose, is still an engineering marvel.
2 Interestingly, InterBase had an architecture that caused disk-writes to leave the database in an always-consistent state. This is one reason that contributes to its ability to recover from hard failures so quickly.

Dwarves, Elves, Wizards, and Kings

Evan Cofsky

IN NEAL STEPHENSON'S NOVEL *CRYPTONOMICON* (EOS), Randy Waterhouse explains his classification system for the different types of people he meets. Dwarves are hard workers, steadily producing beautiful artifacts in the dark loneliness of their caves. They exert tremendous forces moving mountains and shaping earth, and are renowned for their craftsmanship. Elves are elegant, cultured, and spend their days creating new and beautiful magical things. They are so gifted they don't even realize that other races view these things as otherworldly almost. The wizards are immensely powerful beings almost completely unlike all others, but unlike the elves, they do know about magic and its power and nature, and they wield it with supreme effect. But there is a fourth type of character that Waterhouse alludes to but does not mention specifically. The kings are the visionaries who know what must be done with all of these different characters.

An architect is a king of sorts. The architect must be familiar with all of these characters, and ensure that the architecture has roles for all of them. An architecture designed only for one will attract only that one character to the project, and even with the best dwarves, or elves, or wizards, the team will be severely limited in its reach if it can only approach problems in one way.

A good king will lead all types through a quest, and help them work together to complete it. Without the quest, there is no vision for the team, and it ultimately becomes a partisan mess. Without all the characters, the team can only solve one class of problem, and is stopped at the first barrier impassable to that solution.

The architect creates the quest with all the characters in mind. The architecture then becomes a guide for finding tasks for the different characters to perform while learning about one another. When a project encounters difficulty, the team will already know how to approach solving it because the architecture gave them the opportunities to grow into a team.

Evan Cofsky is a software engineer, an amateur musician, and an avid cyclist. He studied both music and computer science in college, and continues to study them. Currently he is a senior software engineer with Virgin Charter as its resident Python expert, and works with an eclectic team of exceptionally bright and diverse people.

Learn from Architects of Buildings

Keith Braithwaite

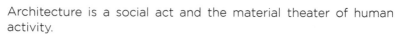

> Architecture is a social act and the material theater of human activity.
>
> *—Spiro Kostof*

HOW MANY SOFTWARE ARCHITECTS see their role as exclusively, or primarily, technical? Is it not rather that they are the conciliators, go-betweens and arbiters of the warring factions among the stake-holders? How many approach their work in a purely intellectual spirit, without giving proper weight to the human factors of their job?

> A great architect is not made by way of a brain nearly so much as he is made by way of a cultivated, enriched heart.
>
> *—Frank Lloyd Wright*

What more strongly marks out the architects in your organization: raw intellectual horsepower and vast capacity to recall technical minutiae, or taste, refinement, and generosity of spirit? Under which tendency would you prefer to work?

> A doctor can bury his mistakes but an architect can only advise his client to plant vines.
>
> *—ibid*

Is the "maintenance" of "legacy" systems anything more than pruning those vines? Would you, as an architect, have the intestinal fortitude to scrap a piece of work that had failed? Or would you cover it up? Wright also said that the architect's best friend was the sledgehammer. What have you demolished recently?

Architects believe that not only do they sit at the right hand of God, but that if God ever gets up, they take the chair.

—Karen Moyer

For "God," read "customer."

In architecture as in all other operative arts, the end must direct the operation. The end is to build well. Well building has three conditions: Commodity, Firmness and Delight.

—Henry Watton

When was the last time you saw a piece of software whose architecture gave you any delight? Do you aim to give delight with your work?

No person who is not a great sculptor or painter can be an architect. If he is not a sculptor or painter, he can only be a builder

—John Ruskin

Does artistry play its proper part in your architecture? Is the assemblage of components to make systems informed by a painterly concern for shape and texture, a sculptural sense of balance and implied motion, or the importance of negative space?

And finally, no gloss is required on this comment, a sure remedy for the software architect's most damaging syndrome.

It seems a fantastic paradox, but it is nevertheless a most important truth, that no architecture can be truly noble which is not imperfect.

—ibid

Author bio available on page 21.

Fight Repetition

Niclas Nilsson

ARE YOUR DEVELOPERS performing recurring tasks that need little thinking? Can you find recurring patterns in the code? Can you spot code that's been written copy-paste-modify style? If that's the case, your team is moving slower than it should and, oddly enough, you may be the cause.

Before explaining why, let's agree on a couple of truths about software development:

- Duplication is evil.

- Repetitive work slows down development.

As an architect, you set the tone. You've got the best overall grasp of the system and you probably wrote a trend-setting, end-to-end, vertical slice of the system that serves as an example for the team—an example that has been copied many times by now. Whenever a developer copies anything—be it a few lines of code, an XML file, or a class—that's a clear indication that something could be made simpler or even completely abstracted away. Most often, it's not the domain logic that is copied; it's the infrastructure code that just has to be there to make it work. For that reason, it's crucial that you can envision the effects your examples have. Any code and configuration in your examples will be the base for tens, hundreds, or maybe thousands of other slices of the system, which means you have to make sure that your code is clean, intention revealing, and containing nothing except what can't be abstracted away: the domain problem itself. As an architect, you need to be highly sensitive to any kind of repetitive patterns, since anything you write will (ironically) be repeated.

But that doesn't happen in your system, right? Take a look at that configuration file. What needs to be different if applied on another slice of the system, and what will stay the same? Look at a typical business layer method. Is there a pattern that shows up in other methods as well, containing things like transaction handling, logging, authentication, or auditing? How about the data access layer? Any code in there that will be the same except for names of entities and fields? Look broader. Can you find two or three lines of code that frequently seem to go together, and even though they operate on different objects, feel like the same thing? These are all examples of repetition. Repetition in code is something that developers eventually learn to filter out and ignore when reading the code, once they figure out where the interesting variabilities are found, but even if the developers get used to it, it slows them down. Code like that is clearly written for computers to execute, not for developers to read.

Your responsibility is to remove it. To do that, you may need to harvest frameworks, create better abstractions, perhaps ask the toolsmith to set up an aspect framework or write a few small code generators, but the repetition won't go away unless someone does something about it.

That someone is you.

Author bio available on page 31.

Welcome to the Real World

Gregor Hohpe

ENGINEERS LIKE PRECISION, especially software engineers who live in the realm of ones and zeros. They are used to working with binary decisions, one or zero, true or false, yes or no. Everything is clear and consistent, guaranteed by foreign key constraints, atomic transactions, and checksums.

Unfortunately, the real world is not quite that binary. Customers place orders, only to cancel them a moment later. Checks bounce, letters are lost, payments delayed, and promises broken. Data entry errors are bound to happen every so often. Users prefer "shallow" user interfaces, which give them access to many functions at once without being boxed into a lengthy, one-dimensional "process," which is easier to program and seems more "logical" to many developers. Instead of the call stack controlling the program flow, the user is in charge.

Worse yet, widely distributed systems introduce a whole new set of inconsistencies into the game. Services may not be reachable, change without prior notice, or do not provide transactional guarantees. When you run applications on thousands of machine, failure is no longer a question of "if," but of "when." These systems are loosely coupled, asynchronous, concurrent, and do not adhere to traditional transaction semantics. You should have taken the blue pill!

As computer scientists' brave new world is crumbling, what are we to do? As is so often the case, awareness is a first important step toward a solution.

Say goodbye to the good old predictive call-stack architecture, where you get to define what happens when and in what order. Instead, be ready to respond to events at any time in any order, regaining your context as needed. Make asynchronous requests concurrently instead of calling methods one by one. Avoid complete chaos by modeling your application using event-driven process chains or state models. Reconcile errors through compensation, retry, or tentative operations.

Sounds scary and more than you bargained for? Luckily, the real world has to deal with the same issues for a long time: delayed letters, broken promises, messages crossing in transit, payments posted to the wrong account—the examples are countless. Accordingly, people had to resend letters, write off bad orders, or tell you to ignore the payment reminder in case you already sent a payment. So don't just blame the real world for your headaches, but also use it as a place to look for solutions. After all, Starbucks does not two-phase commit, either.[1] Welcome to the real world.

> *Gregor Hohpe is a software architect with Google, Inc. Gregor is a widely recognized thought leader on asynchronous messaging architectures and service-oriented architectures. He coauthored the seminal book* Enterprise Integration Patterns *(Addison-Wesley Professional) and speaks regularly at technical conferences around the world.*

1 See *http://www.eaipatterns.com/ramblings/18_starbucks.html.*

Don't Control, but Observe

Gregor Hohpe

TODAY'S SYSTEMS ARE DISTRIBUTED AND LOOSELY COUPLED. Building loosely coupled systems is a bit of a drag, so why do we bother? Because we want our systems to be flexible so they do not break apart at the slightest change. This is a critical property in today's environments, where we may only control a small portion of our application, the remainder living in distributed services or third-party packages, controlled by other departments or external vendors.

So, it looks like the effort to build a system that is flexible and can evolve over time is a good idea. But that also means our system will change over time. As in "today's system is not what it was yesterday." Unfortunately, this makes documenting the system challenging. It's commonly known that documentation is out of date the moment it is printed, but in a system that changes all the time, things can only be worse. Moreover, building a system that is flexible generally means the architecture is more complex and it's more difficult to get the proverbial "big picture." For example, if all system components communicate with one another over logical, configurable channels, one better have a look at the channel configuration to get any idea what is going on. Sending messages into the logical la-la-land is unlikely to trigger a compiler error, but it is sure to disappoint the user whose action was encapsulated in that message.

Being a control-freak architect is so yesteryear, leading to tightly coupled and brittle solutions. But letting the software run wild is sure to spawn chaos. You have to supplement the lack of control with other mechanisms to avoid doing an instrument flight without the instruments. But what kind of instruments do we have? Plenty, actually. Today's programming languages support reflection, and almost all runtime platforms provide runtime metrics. As your system becomes more configurable, the current system configuration is another great source of information. Because so much raw data is difficult to understand, extract a model from it. For example, once you figure out which components send messages to which logical channels, and which components listen to these channels, you can create a graph model of the actual communication between components. You can do this every few minutes or hours, providing an accurate and up-to-date image of the system as it evolves. Think of it as "Reverse MDA."[1] Instead of a model driving the architecture, you build a flexible architecture, and extract the model from the actual system state.

In many cases, it's easy to visualize this model, creating the literal big picture. However, resist the temptation to plot the 3×5-meter billboard of boxes and lines, which contains every class in your system. That picture may pass as contemporary art, but it's not a useful software model. Instead, use a 1,000-foot view as described by Erik Doernenburg, a level of abstraction that actually tells you something. On top of that, you can make sure your model passes basic validation rules, such as the absence of circular dependencies in a dependency graph, or no messages being sent to a logical channel no one listens to.

Letting go of control is a scary thing, even when it comes to system architecture. But supplemented by observation, model extraction, and validation, it is probably the way only to architect for the 21st century.

Author bio available on page 95.

1 MDA = model-driven architecture.

Janus the Architect

David Bartlett

IN THE ROMAN WORLD, Janus was the god of beginnings and endings, doors and passageways. Janus is usually depicted with two heads facing in different directions, a symbol you may have seen on coins or in the movies. Janus represents transitions and changes in life from past to future, young to old, marriage, births, and coming of age.

For any architect, software or structural, Janus's ability to see forward and backward or past to future is a highly regarded skill. An architect strives to merge realities with vision; past success with future direction; business and management expectations with development constraints. Creating these bridges is a major part of being an architect. Often an architect may feel she is trying to span chasms while bringing a project to completion because of different forces acting on a project—for example, ease of access versus security or satisfying present business processes while designing for management's future vision. A good architect must have those two heads capable of carrying two different ideas or thoughts, different goals or visions, to create a product that will satisfy the various project stakeholders.

You should notice that Janus has two heads, not simply two faces. This allows Janus to have the extra ears and eyes needed for awareness. An excellent IT architect will be a superior listener and evaluator. Understanding the reason for a capital expenditure is crucial to determining the goals and vision a management team has for the future of its organization. Being able to evaluate the technical skills of your staff with the design and technology to be used within the project will aid in creating the proper training and programming pairs to ensure a successful project. Knowing what open source solutions to use in combination with common off-the-shelf software can greatly streamline a project's timelines and budgets. An excellent architect will be aware of many of these disparate pieces of the development process and use them to be successful in the project lifecycle.

There are managers who demand and expect godlike qualities from their architects, but that is not the purpose of this comparison. A good architect is open to new ideas, tools and designs that progress the project, team, or profession; she doesn't want to spend most of her time in management meetings or doing all the coding; she should concede to good ideas and cultivate an atmosphere for ideas to grow. It is an open mind that will succeed in architecture; a mind that can balance the many conflicting forces at work on projects. All architects strive to complete their projects and ensure the success of their development teams. The best architects create systems that stand the test of time because these systems are able to be maintained and expanded into the future as the organization grows and technology changes. These architects have listened, evaluated, and refactored their processes, designs, and methods to ensure the success of their work and projects; they have endeavored to ensure their products will withstand the transitions and changes that are sure to come.

This is the mindset we should strive for as architects. It is simple yet difficult to perform. Like Janus, a software architect needs to be a keeper of doors and passageways, spanning the old and the new, incorporating creativity with sound engineering to fulfill today's requirements while planning to meet tomorrow's expectations.

Author bio available on page 41.

Architects' Focus Is on the Boundaries and Interfaces

Einar Landre

SINCE LORD NELSON DESTROYED the French and Spanish fleet at Trafalgar in 1805, "divide and conquer" has been the mantra for dealing with complex and difficult problems. A more familiar term with the same intent is *separation of concern*. From separation of concern we get encapsulation, and from encapsulation we get boundaries and interfaces.

From an architect's point of view, the hard part is to find the natural places to locate boundaries and define the appropriate interfaces needed to build a working system. This is especially difficult in large enterprise systems, often characterized by few natural boundaries and intertangled domains. In this situation, old wisdom such as "Minimize coupling, maximize cohesion" and "Do not slice through regions where high rates of information exchange are required" provide some guidance, but they say nothing about how to communicate the problems and potential solutions to stakeholders in a easy way.

Here the concept of bounded contexts and context mapping, as described by Eric Evans in his book *Domain-Driven Design* (Addison-Wesley Professional), comes to the rescue. A bounded context is an area where a model or concept is uniquely defined, and we represent it as a cloud or bubble with a descriptive name that defines its role and responsibility in the domain at hand. As an example, a shipping system might include contexts such as Cargo Operation, Cargo Scheduling, and Harbor Movement. In other domains, other names will be appropriate.

With the bounded contexts identified and drawn up on the whiteboard, it's time to start to draw the relationships between the contexts. These relationships might address organizational, functional, or technical dependencies. The result from this exercise is a context map, a collection of bounded contexts and the interfaces between them.

Such a context map provides architects with a powerful tool that allows them to focus on what belongs together and what should be kept apart, enabling them to divide and conquer wisely in a communicative way. The technique can easily be used to document and analyze the as-is situation, and from there guide redesign toward a better system characterized by low coupling, high cohesion, and well-defined interfaces.

Author bio available on page 13.

Empower Developers

Timothy High

THINGS ARE USUALLY EASIER SAID THAN DONE, and software architects are notoriously good at coming up with things to say. To keep your words from becoming a lot of hot air (generally the key ingredient in making vaporware), you need a good team of developers. The role of an architect is usually to impose constraints, but you also have the opportunity to be an enabler. To the extent your responsibilities allow, you should do everything possible to empower your developers.

Make sure developers have the tools they need. Tools shouldn't be imposed on developers, they should be carefully chosen to make sure they are the right tools for the job at hand. Repetitive and mindless work should be automated wherever possible. Also, it is well worth the investment to make sure developers have top-notch machines to work with, adequate network bandwidth, and access to software, data, and information necessary to carry out their work.

Make sure they have the skills they need. If training is required, make sure they get it. Invest in books and promote active discussions about technology. The work life of a developer should be hands-on and practical, but also should be actively academic. If you have the budget for it, send your team to technical presentations and conferences. If not, get them involved in technical mailing lists and look for free events in your city. As much as possible, participate in the developer selection process as well. Look for developers that are hungry to learn, that have that little "spark" that says they really dig technology (also make sure they can play ball with the team…). It's hard to get a big bang out of a team of duds.

Let developers make their own decisions wherever it won't contradict the overall goal of the software design. But put constraints where they count, not only to guarantee quality, but also to further empower developers. Create standards for the sake of consistency, but also to reduce the number of troublesome, insignificant decisions that aren't part of the essential problem developers are solving. Create a clear roadmap for where to put their source files, what to call them, when to create new ones, and so on. This will save them time.

Lastly, protect developers from nonessential parts of their job. Too much paperwork and too many office chores add overhead and reduce their effectiveness. You (usually) aren't a manager, but you can have influence on the processes surrounding software development. Whatever processes are used, make sure they are designed to remove obstacles, not increase them.

Timothy High is a software architect with more than 15 years' experience with web, multitiered client-server, and application-integration technologies. He is currently working as a software architect for Sakonnet Technologies, a leader in Energy Trading and Risk Management (ETRM) software.

Record Your Rationale

Timothy High

THERE IS MUCH DEBATE in the software development community about the value of documentation, especially with regard to the design of the software itself. The disagreements generally cluster around the perceived value of doing a "big upfront design," and the difficulties of maintaining design documentation synchronized with an ever-changing code base.

One type of documentation that ages well, doesn't require much effort, and almost always pays off is a record of the rationale behind decisions that are made regarding the software architecture. As explained in Mark Richards's axiom "Architectural Tradeoffs," the definition of a software architecture is all about choosing the right tradeoffs between various quality attributes, cost, time, and other factors. It should be made clear to you, your managers, developers, and other software stakeholders why one solution was chosen over another and what tradeoffs this entailed. (Did you sacrifice horizontal scalability in the name of reducing hardware and licensing costs? Was security such a concern that it was acceptable to increase the overall response time in exchange for data encryption?)

The exact format of this documentation can vary according to what is appropriate for your project, from quick notes in a text document, wiki, or blog, to using a more formal template to record all aspects of each architectural decision. Whatever the form and format, the documentation should answer the basic questions "What was that decision we made?", and "Why did we make that decision?". A secondary question that is often asked and should be documented is "What other solutions were considered, and why were they rejected?" (actually, the question usually asked is, "Why can't we do it *my* way?"). The documentation should also be searchable so that you can easily find it whenever it's needed.

This documentation may come in handy in a number of situations:

- As a means of communication to developers regarding important architectural principles that should be followed

- To get the team "on the same page," or even head off a mutiny, when developers question the logic behind the architecture (or even to humbly accept criticism if it turns out a decision doesn't hold up under scrutiny)

- To show managers and stakeholders exactly why the software is being built the way it is (such as why an expensive piece of hardware or software is necessary)

- When handing off the project to a new architect (how many times have you inherited a piece of software and wondered exactly why the designers did it THAT way?)

However, the most important benefits that come from this practice are:

- It forces you to be explicit about your reasoning in order to verify that your foundations are solid (see the next axiom "Challenge Assumptions— Especially Your Own").

- It can be used as a starting point to re-evaluate a decision when the conditions that influenced it have changed.

The effort required to create this documentation is equivalent to jotting down a few notes whenever you have a meeting or discussion on the subject. Whatever the format you choose, this is one type of documentation that is worth the investment.

Author bio available on page 103.

Challenge Assumptions— Especially Your Own

Timothy High

WETHERN'S LAW OF SUSPENDED JUDGMENT STATES (in a rather tongue-in-cheek fashion) that "Assumption is the mother of all screw-ups." A more popular take on this would be, "Don't assume—it makes an 'ass' of 'u' and 'me.'" But when you are dealing with assumptions that could cost thousands, if not millions, of dollars it's not always a laughing matter.

Best practices in software architecture state that you should document the rationale behind each decision that is made, especially when that decision involves a tradeoff (performance versus maintainability, cost versus time-to-market, and so on). In more formal approaches, it is common to record along with each decision the context of that decision, including the "factors" that contributed to the final judgment. Factors may be functional or nonfunctional requirements, but they also may just be "facts" (or factoids...) that the decision-makers found important (technology constraints, available skill sets, the political environment, etc.).

This practice is valuable because listing these factors helps highlight assumptions that the architects may have that affect important decisions about the software being designed. Very often these assumptions are based on "historical reasons," opinion, developer lore, FUDs, or even "something I heard in the hallway":

- "Open source is not reliable."
- "Bitmap indexes are more trouble than they're worth."
- "The customer would *never* accept a page that takes five seconds to load."
- "The CIO would reject anything that isn't sold by a major vendor."

It is important to make these assumptions visible and explicit for the sake of posterity and for future re-evaluation. However, it is even more critical to make sure that any assumptions that aren't based on relevant empirical evidence (or a confirmation from the people involved, for political factors) be validated before a decision is finalized. What if customers can wait five seconds for critical reports if you provide a counter? In exactly what way is exactly which open source project unreliable? Have you tested the bitmap indexes on your data, using your application's transactions and queries?

And don't overlook the word "relevant." Something that was true in an older version of your software may not be true today. The performance of bitmap indexes in one version of Oracle may not be the same as in another. An older version of a library may have had security holes that have already been fixed. Your old reliable software vendor may be on its last legs financially. The technology landscape changes every day, and so do people. Who knows? Maybe your CIO has become a closet fan of Linux.

Facts and assumptions are the pillars on which your software will be built. Whatever they are, make sure the foundations are solid.

Author bio available on page 103.

Share Your Knowledge and Experiences

Paul W. Homer

FROM ALL OF OUR EXPERIENCES, including both success and failure, we learn a great deal. In a young industry like software development, disseminating this experience and knowledge is vital in helping sustain progress. What each team learns in its own tiny little corner of the world is possibly influential across the globe.

Realistically our fundamental knowledge base for software development—that is, the knowledge that is absolute and theoretically correct—is small compared to what is necessary to successfully develop a project. To compensate, we guess, rely on intuitive judgments or even pick randomly. In that, any major development project generates empirical evidence into what works and what fails. We're gradually working through the permutations, which we want to apply back to the industry as a whole.

At an individual level, we are all trying to grow and come to understand how to build larger and larger systems. The course of our careers will take us toward ever-increasing challenges, for which we want our past experiences to help guide us. Being there is one thing, but to get the most from the experience we often have to rationalize it. The best and easiest way of working through it is to attempt to explain it to another person.

The act of discussing something always helps to show its weaknesses. You don't really understand something until you can explain it easily. It's only by putting forth our explanations and discussing them that we solidify the experience into knowledge.

Another point is that while we may have had specific experiences, the inferences we draw from them may not be entirely correct in the overall context. We may not have been as successful as we thought, or as smart as we wanted. Of course, testing your knowledge against the real world is scary, particularly when you find out that something dear is myth, incorrect, or was never true; it's hard to be wrong.

Ultimately, we are human beings so not everything in our minds is correct; not every thought we have is reasonable. It's only when we accept our flaws that we open up the possibility of improving. The old adage about learning more from failure always holds. If our ideas and beliefs do not stand the test of a debate, then it is better we find out now than build on it later.

We really want to share our knowledge and experience to help the industry progress; we also realize it helps us to understand and correct it. Given the state of so much of our software, it is clearly important for us to take every opportunity to share the things we know, what we think we know, and what we've seen. If we help those around us to improve, they'll help us to reach our full potential.

> *Paul W. Homer is a software developer, writer, and occasional photographer, who was drawn into software development several decades ago and has been struggling ever since with trying to build increasingly complex systems.*

Pattern Pathology

Chad LaVigne

DESIGN PATTERNS ARE ONE OF THE MOST VALUABLE TOOLS available to the software architect. Using patterns allows us to create common solutions that are easier to communicate and understand. They are concepts that are directly associated with good design. This fact can make it very enticing to demonstrate our architectural prowess by throwing a lot of patterns at a project. If you find yourself trying to shoehorn your favorite patterns into a problem space where they don't apply, you may be a victim of pattern pathology.

Many projects suffer from this condition. These are the projects where you envision the original architect looking up from the last page in his patterns book, rubbing his hands together and saying, "Now, which one will I use first!?". This mentality is somewhat akin to that of a developer who begins writing a class with the thought "hmmm, what class should I extend?". Design patterns are excellent tools for mitigating necessary complexity, but like all tools, they can be misused. Design patterns become a problem when we make them the proverbial hammer with which we must strike every nail. Be careful that your appreciation for patterns doesn't become an infatuation that has you introducing solutions that are more complicated than they need to be.

Stamping patterns all over a project unnecessarily is over-engineering. Design patterns are not magic and using them doesn't automatically qualify a solution as good design. They are reusable solutions to recurring problems. They have been discovered and documented by others to help us recognize when we're looking at a wheel that's already been invented. It's our job to identify problems solved by these solutions when they arise and apply design patterns appropriately. Don't let your desire to exhibit design pattern knowledge cloud your pragmatic vision. Keep your sights focused on designing systems that provide effective business solutions and use patterns to solve the problems they address.

Chad LaVigne is a solutions architect and technical hired gun for Baltimore-based TEKSystems, Inc. He works primarily in the Minneapolis area designing and implementing solutions utilizing Enterprise Java technologies.

Don't Stretch the Architecture Metaphors

David Ing

ARCHITECTS LIKE TO DEAL WITH METAPHORS. They provide nice concrete handles on subjects that are often abstract, complex, and moving targets. Whether it is communicating with the rest of the team or talking through the architecture with the end user, it is so tempting to find something tangible or physical to use as a metaphor for what you are trying to build.

This usually starts well, in that a common language can evolve where people start to feel that things are moving in the right direction. The metaphor develops and grows over time until it takes on a life of its own. People feel good about the metaphor—we're making progress!

What usually happens is that the metaphor for the architecture now becomes dangerous. Here's how it can turn on its architect creators:

- The business domain customer starts to like your metaphor more that your proposed system, in that the happiest possible interpretation is now shared by all concerned and no real constraints are uncovered.

Example: "We're building a transport system like a ship travelling between a series of docks."

You think container ships crossing the Pacific. I was actually thinking a rowing boat in a swimming pool, with possibly one oar.

- The development team starts to think that the metaphor is more important than the actual business problem. You start to justify odd decisions because of a fondness for the metaphor.

Example: "We said it's like a filing cabinet, so of course we have to show it to the user alphabetically. I know it's a filing cabinet with six dimensions and of infinite length and with a clock built in to it, but we've done the icon now—so it has to be a filing cabinet…".

- The delivered system contains relics of names from old, broken metaphors long gone—archaeological testimonials to concepts long refactored and dug over.

Example: "Why does the Billing Factory object create a Port channel for the Rowing boat system? Surely it should return a Pomegranate view for the Hub Bus? What do you mean you're new here?"

So remember, don't fall in love with your system metaphor—only use it for exploratory communication purposes, and don't let it turn on you.

David Ing is a software architect/technologist living and working in Vancouver, British Columbia. Originally from the U.K., he moved across to get away from the rain, although now feels tricked by dishonest tourist literature.

As fashion dictates, he now works at Web 2.0 company Taglocity, where he splits his time trying to make email systems "less awful" and figure out what Web 2.0 actually means.

Focus on Application Support and Maintenance

Mncedisi Kasper

THE SUPPORT AND MAINTENANCE OF AN APPLICATION should never, ever be an afterthought. Since over 80% of an application's lifecycle is spent in maintenance, you should pay a lot of attention to the problems of support and maintenance when you're designing. Fail to heed this, and you'll watch with horror as your application stops being the architect's dream and becomes a vile beast that dies a horrible death and is forever remembered as a failure.

When most architects design applications, they think mainly of developers, who have IDEs and debuggers in place. If something goes wrong, highly skilled software engineers debug away and the bug is discovered. It's easy to think this way because most architects have spent most of their lives as developers rather than administrators. Unfortunately, the developer and the support guy have different skill sets, just as the development/testing environment and the production environment have different purposes.

Here are a few of the disadvantages that an administrator faces:

- An administrator can't resubmit a request message to reproduce the problem. When you're in production, you can't reissue a financial transaction against the "live" database to see what went wrong.

- Once the application is in production, the pressure to fix bugs comes from customers and executives, not from the project manager and the testing team—and an angry CEO can be a lot more threatening.

- Once you're in production, there is no debugger.

- Once you're in production, deployment needs to be scheduled and coordinated. You can't take a production application down for a few minutes to test a bug fix.

- The logging level is much higher in the development environment than in production.

A few symptoms of this failure to plan for support are:

- Most problems require a developer's involvement.
- The relationship between the development team and the support team is sour; the developers think the support team is a bunch of idiots.
- The support team hates the new application.
- The architect and development teams are spending a lot of time in production.
- The application is restarted often as a way to resolve problems.
- The administrators never have time to tune the system properly because they're always fighting fires.

To ensure that your application succeeds once it's out of the developers' hands, you should:

- Understand that development and support require a different skill set.
- Get a support lead as early in on the project as possible.
- Make the support lead a core part of the team.
- Involve a support lead with the planning for the application support.

Design such that the learning curve for the support personnel is minimal. Traceability, auditing, and logging are crucial. When the administrators are happy, everybody is happy (especially your boss).

Mncedisi Kasper is a director of technology and strategy at Open Xcellence ICT Solutions, a South Africa–based company specializing in enterprise application integration and SAP (ABAP/XI) consultancy.

Prepare to Pick Two

Bill de hÓra

SOMETIMES ACCEPTING A CONSTRAINT or giving up on a property can lead to a better architecture, one that is easier and less expensive to build and run. Like buses, desirable properties tend to come in threes, and trying to define and build a system that supports all three can result in a system that does nothing especially well.

A famous example is Brewer's conjecture, also known as Consistency, Availability, and Partitioning (CAP), which states that there are three properties that are commonly desired in a distributed system—consistency, availability, and partition tolerance—and that it is impossible to achieve all three. Trying to have all three will drastically increase the engineering costs and typically increase complexity without actually achieving the desired effect or business goal. If your data must be available and distributed, achieving consistency becomes increasingly expensive and eventually impossible. Likewise, if the system must be distributed and consistent, ensuring consistency will lead at first to latency and performance problems and eventually to unavailability since the system cannot be exposed as it tries to reaches agreement.

It's often the case that one or more properties are considered inviolate: data cannot be duplicated, all writes must be transactional, the system must be

100% available, calls must be asynchronous, there must be no single point of failure, everything must be extensible, and so on. Apart from being naïve, treating properties as religious artifacts will stop you from thinking about the problem at hand. We start to talk about architectural deviation instead of principled design and we confuse dogmatism with good governance. Instead we should ask, why must these properties hold? What benefit is to be had by doing so? When are these properties desirable? How can we break up the system to achieve a better result? Be ever the skeptic, because architectural dogma tends to undermine delivery. The inevitability of such tradeoffs is one of the most difficult things to accept in software development, not just as architects, but also as developers and stakeholders. But we should cherish them; it's far better than having limitless choice, and accepting tradeoffs often induces a creative and inventive result.

> *Bill de hÓra is chief architect with NewBay Software, where he works on large scale web and mobile systems. He is co-editor of the Atom Publishing Protocol and previously served on the W3C RDF Working Group. He is a recognized expert on REST style and message-passing architectures and protocol design.*

Prefer Principles, Axioms, and Analogies to Opinion and Taste

Michael Harmer

WHEN CREATING YOUR ARCHITECTURE you should explicitly use principles, axioms, and analogies to guide the creation. This gives the architecture a number of benefits that are not present if you simply create by implicitly leveraging your experience, opinions, and tastes.

Documenting your architecture will be easier. You can start by describing the principles that were followed. This is much easier than trying to communicate your opinions and experience. The principles will then provide a convenient handle for those tasked with understanding and implementing the architecture. It will also be invaluable for subsequent or inexperienced architects who need to work with the architecture.

An architecture with clear principles is an architecture that frees its architect from reviewing everything and being everywhere. It gives architects greater leverage and influence. You will not need to be an omniscient workaholic to ensure that others can consistently:

- Implement and adapt the architecture
- Extend the architecture into related domains
- Reimplement the architecture using newer technologies
- Work out the detailed edge cases

Disagreements about opinion and taste invariably turn into political arguments in which authority is used to win. However, disagreements where the foundation principles are clear provide a way for more reasoned discussion to occur without issues being personalised. It also allows the disagreements to be resolved without reference to the architect at all.

Principles and axioms also give an architecture consistency throughout its implementation and across time. Consistency is often a problem, especially in large systems that span multiple technologies and will exist for many years. Clear architectural principles allow those unfamiliar with a particular technology or component to reason about and more readily understand the unfamiliar technology.

Michael Harmer has worked in software for 16 years as a developer, team leader, architect, principal engineer, and practice manager.

Start with a Walking Skeleton

Clint Shank

ONE VERY USEFUL STRATEGY FOR IMPLEMENTING, verifying, and evolving an application architecture is to start with what Alistair Cockburn calls a *walking skeleton*. A walking skeleton is a minimal, end-to-end implementation of the system that links together all the main architectural components. Starting small, with a working system exercising all the communication paths, gives you confidence that you are heading in the right direction.

Once the skeleton is in place, it's time to put it on a workout program. Bulk it up with full body workouts. This means implement incrementally, adding end-to-end functionality. The goal is to keep the system running, all the while growing the skeleton.

Making changes to an architecture is harder and more expensive the longer it has been around and the bigger it gets. We want to find mistakes early. This approach gives us a short feedback cycle from which we can more quickly adapt and work iteratively as necessary to meet the business's prioritized list of runtime-discernable quality attributes. Assumptions about the architecture are validated earlier. The architecture is more easily evolved because problems are found at an earlier stage when less has been invested in its implementation.

The bigger the system, the more important it is to use this strategy. In a small application, one developer can implement a feature from top to bottom relatively quickly, but this becomes impractical with larger systems. It is quite common to have multiple developers on a single team or even on multiple, possibly distributed, teams involved in implementing end-to-end. Consequently, more coordination is necessary. And naturally, developers implement at a different pace. Some developers can accomplish a lot and in little time while others can spend a lot of time implementing very little. More difficult and time consuming efforts should be done earlier in the project.

Start with a walking skeleton, keep it running, and grow it incrementally.

Clint Shank is a software developer, consultant, and mentor at Sphere of Influence, Inc., a software design and engineering services company for commercial and federal clients.

It Is All About The Data

Paul W. Homer

AS SOFTWARE DEVELOPERS we initially understand software as a system of commands, functions, and algorithms. This instruction-oriented view of software aids us in learning how to build software, but it is this very same perspective that starts to hamper us when we try to build bigger systems.

If you stand back a little, a computer is nothing more than a fancy tool to help you access and manipulate piles of data. It is the structure of this data that lies at the heart of understanding how to manage complexity in a huge system. Millions of instructions are intrinsically complicated, but underneath we can easily get our brains around a smaller set of basic data structures.

For instance, if you want to understand the Unix operating system, digging through the source code line-by-line is unlikely to help. If, however, you read a book outlining the primary internal data structures for handling things like processes and the filesystem, you'll have a better chance of understanding how UNIX works underneath. The data is conceptually smaller than the code and considerably less complicated.

As code is running in a computer, the underlying state of the data is continually changing. In an abstract sense, we can see any algorithm as being just a simple transformation from one version of the data to another. We can see all functionality as just a larger set of well-defined transformations pushing the data through different revisions.

This data-oriented perspective—seeing the system entirely by the structure of its underlying information—can reduce even the most complicated system down to a tangible collection of details. A reduction in complexity is necessary for understanding how to build and run complex systems.

Data sits at the core of most problems. Business domain problems creep into the code via the data. Most key algorithms, for example, are often well understood; it is the structure and relationships of the data that frequently change. Operational issues like upgrades are also considerably more difficult if they affect data. This happens because changing code or behavior is not a big issue, it just needs to be released, but revising data structures can involve a huge effort in transforming the old version into a newer one.

And of course, many of the base problems in software architecture are really about data. Is the system collecting the right data at the right time, and who should be able to see or modify it? If the data exists, what is its quality and how fast is it growing? If not, what is its structure, and where does it reliably come from? In this light, once the data is in the system, the only other question is whether or not there is already a way to view and/or edit the specific data, or does that need to be added?

From a design perspective, the critical issue for most systems is to get the right data into the system at the right time. From there, applying different transformations to the data is a matter of making it available, executing the functionality, and then saving the results. Most systems don't have to be particularly complex underneath in order for them to work, they just need to build up bigger and bigger piles of data. Functionality is what we see first, but it's data that forms the core of every system.

Author bio available on page 109.

Make Sure the Simple Stuff Is Simple

Chad LaVigne

SOFTWARE ARCHITECTS SOLVE a lot of very difficult problems but we also solve some relatively easy ones. What we don't want to do is apply a complicated solution to an easy problem. As obvious as that advice sounds, it can be hard follow. People who design software are smart—really smart. The simple problem–complex solution trap can be an easy one to fall into because we like to demonstrate our knowledge. If you find yourself designing a solution so clever that it may become self-aware, stop and think. Does the solution fit the problem? If the answer is no, reconsider your design options. Keep the simple stuff simple. You'll get plenty of chances to showcase your talent when the difficult problems arise, and they will.

This doesn't mean that we shouldn't implement elegant solutions. It means that if we're tasked with designing a system that only needs to support selling one type of SKU-based widget, it's probably a bad idea to design for hierarchies of dynamically configurable products.

The cost incurred by a complicated solution may seem small, but chances are that it's larger than you're giving it credit for. Over-engineering at the architectural level causes many of the same issues as it does at the development level, but the negative effects tend to be multiplied. Poor decisions made at the design level are more difficult to implement, maintain, and—worst of all—reverse. Before moving forward with an architectural decision that exceeds system requirements, ask yourself how difficult it would be to remove after it's in place.

The costs don't stop with the implementation and maintenance of the solution in question. Spending more time than necessary on an easy problem leaves less time for when the complicated issues show up. Suddenly your architecture decisions are creating scope creep and adding unnecessary risk to the project. Your time could be spent much more efficiently making sure no one else is doing that.

There's often a strong desire to justify solutions with a perceived benefit or implied requirements. Remember this: when you try to guess at future requirements, 50% of the time you're wrong and 49% of the time you're very, very wrong. Solve today's problem today. Get the application out the door on time and wait for feedback to generate real requirements. The simple design you create will make it much easier to integrate those new requirements when they arrive. If you beat the odds and your implied requirement becomes a real one on the next release, you'll already have a solution in mind. The difference is that now you'll be able to allocate appropriate time for it in the estimate because it's truly required. Before you know it, you've got the reputation of a team that makes good estimates and gets work done on time.

Author bio available on page 111.

Before Anything, an Architect Is a Developer

Mike Brown

HAVE YOU HEARD OF A JUDGE WHO WASN'T A LAWYER, or a chief of surgery who wasn't a surgeon? Even after they get to what some would call the pinnacles of their career, the people holding these occupations are still expected to continue learning the new developments within their respective fields. As software architects, we should be held to the same standards.

No matter how well designed a solution is, one of the most important factors for determining the success of an implementation is getting the developers to sign on to the game plan. The quickest way to get the developers to sign on is to gain their respect and trust. We all know the quickest way to gain a developer's trust: *your code is your currency*. If you can show your developers that you're not just some pie-in-the-sky daydreamer who can't code his way out of a paper bag, you'll hear less grumbling about the hoops you're "making" them jump through to get data to show on the page when "I can get it done in less time by just binding a dataset to a grid."

Even though I'm not required to as part of my job, I will frequently pick up some of the more intricate tasks. This serves two purposes: first it's fun and helps me to keep my development skills sharp; second, it helps me demonstrate to my developers that I'm not just blowing smoke where the sun doesn't shine.

As an architect, your primary goal should be to create a solution that is feasible, maintainable, and of course addresses the issue at hand. Part of knowing what is feasible in a solution is having knowledge of the effort involved in developing the elements of the solution. Therefore, I propose that *if you design it, you should be able to code it.*

Mike Brown is a lead software engineer for Software Engineering Professionals, Inc. (http://www.sep.com). He has 13 years of experience in IT, including 8 years' experience developing enterprise solutions in a wide range of vertical markets. He is a founder of the Indianapolis Alt.NET user group, a charter member of the WPF Disciples, and organizer of the upcoming Indy Arc professional user group.

The ROI Variable

George Malamidis

EVERY DECISION WE MAKE FOR OUR PROJECTS, be it technology-, process- or people-related, can be a viewed as a form of investment. Investments come associated with a cost, which may or may not be monetary, and carry trust that they will eventually pay off. Our employers choose to offer us salaries in the hope that this investment will positively affect the outcome of their venture. We decide to follow a specific development methodology in the hope that it will make the team more productive. We choose to spend a month redesigning the physical architecture of an application in the belief that it will be beneficial in the long run.

One of the ways of measuring the success of investments is by rate of return, also known as *return on investment* (ROI). For example, "we anticipate that by spending more time writing tests, we will have fewer bugs in our next production release." The cost of the investment in this case is derived from the time spent writing tests. What we gain is the time saved from fixing bugs in the future, plus the satisfied customers experiencing better-behaved software. Let's assume that currently 10 out of 40 working hours in a week are spent fixing bugs. We estimate that by devoting four hours a week to testing, we will reduce the amount of time spent on fixing bugs to two a week, effectively saving eight hours to invest in something else. The anticipated ROI is 200%, equal to the eight hours we save from bug fixing divided by the four hours we invest in testing.

Not everything need directly translate in monetary gains, but our investments should result in added value. If, for our current project, time to market is essential to the stakeholders, maybe a bulletproof architecture requiring a lengthy upfront design phase will not offer ROI as interesting as a swift alpha release. By quickly going live, we're able to adapt to audience reactions that can form the deciding element for the future direction and success of the project, whereas not thoroughly planning can incur the cost of not being able to scale the application easily enough when the need arises. The ROI of each option can be determined by examining its costs and projected profits, and can be used as a base for selection from available options.

Consider architectural decisions as investments and take into account the associated rate of return; it is a useful approach for finding out how pragmatic or appropriate every option on the table is.

George Malamidis is a software engineer working for TrafficBroker in London. Before that, he was a lead consultant and technical lead at ThoughtWorks. He has helped deliver critical applications in a variety of domains, from networking to banking to Web 2.0.

Your System Is Legacy; Design for It

Dave Anderson

EVEN IF YOUR SYSTEM IS BLEEDING EDGE and developed in the latest technology, it will be legacy to the next guy. Deal with it! The nature of software today means things go out of date fast. If you expect your system to go into production and survive, even for a few months, then you need to accept that maintenance developers will need to fix things up. This means several things:

- Clarity: It should be obvious what role components and classes perform.

- Testability: Is your system easy to verify?

- Correctness: Do things work as designed or as they should? Eliminate quick and nasty fixes.

- Traceability: Can Ernie the Emergency Bug Fixer—who has never seen the code before—jump into production, diagnose a fault, and put in a fix? Or does he need an eight-week handover?

Try to think of a different team opening up the codebase and working out what's happening. This is fundamental for great architecture. It doesn't have to be oversimplified or documented to the hilt; a good design will document itself in many ways. The way a system behaves in production can also expose the design. For example, a sprawling architecture with ugly dependencies will often behave like a caged animal in production. Spare a thought for (usually more junior) developers who may have to debug defects.

Legacy tends to be a bad word in software circles, but in reality, all software systems should endure the tag. It is not a bad thing, as it may indicate that your system is durable, meets expectations, and has business value. Any software system that has never been called legacy has probably been canned before launch—which is not the sign of a successful architecture.

> *Dave Anderson is a principal software engineer at Belfast software company Liberty IT, which supplies IT solutions for Fortune 100 company Liberty Mutual. Dave has more than 10 years' experience in the software industry with many leading-edge IT companies across several different industries and countries.*

If There Is Only One Solution, Get a Second Opinion

Timothy High

YOU'VE PROBABLY HEARD THIS SAID BEFORE. If you're an experienced architect, you know it's true: if you can only think of one solution to a problem, you're in trouble.

Software architecture is about finding the best possible solution for a problem given any number of constraints. It is rarely possible to satisfy all requirements and constraints with the first solution that comes to mind. Generally, tradeoffs must be made by choosing the solution that best satisfies the requirements according to the most critical priorities.

If you only have one solution to the problem at hand, it means that you will have no room to negotiate these tradeoffs. It's very possible that this one solution will be insatisfactory to the stakeholders of your system. It also means that if priorities are shifted due to a changing business environment, your system may have no room to adapt to new requirements.

Rarely, if ever, is this situation caused by a real lack of options. It is much more likely due to the inexperience of the architect in this particular problem domain. If you know this is the case, do yourself a favor and ask someone more experienced to give you a hand.

A more insidious manifestation of this problem is when an architecture is designed from habit. An architect can be experienced with a single style of architecture (e.g., a three-tier, layered client-server system), but not know enough to recognize when that style doesn't fit. If you find yourself in the situation where you automatically *know* the solution, without having done any comparison to other approaches, stop, take a step back, and ask yourself if you can think of another way to do it. If you can't, you may be in need of some help.

A friend of mine was once the technical person in charge of a small, but growing, Internet startup. As its user base started growing, so did the load requirements on its system. Performance was going down the tubes, and the company was starting to lose some of its hard-won user base.

So, the boss asked him, "What can we do to improve the performance?"

My friend had the answer: "Buy a bigger machine!"

"What else can we do?"

"Umm...as far as I know, that's it."

My friend was fired on the spot. Of course, the boss was right.

Author bio available on page 103.

Understand the Impact of Change

Doug Crawford

A GOOD ARCHITECT REDUCES COMPLEXITY TO A MINIMUM and can design a solution whose abstractions provide solid foundations to build upon, but are pragmatic enough to weather change.

The great architect understands the impact of change—not just in isolated software modules, but also between people and between systems.

Change can manifest in a variety of forms:

- Functional requirements change

- Scalability needs evolve

- System interfaces are modified

- People in the team come and go

- And the list goes on…

The breadth and complexity of change in a software project is impossible to fathom upfront, and it's a fruitless task trying to accommodate every potential bump before it happens. But the architect can play a crucial role in determining whether the bumps in the road make or break a project.

The architect's role is not necessarily to manage change, but rather to ensure that change is manageable.

Take, for example, a highly distributed solution that spans many applications and relies on a variety of middleware to glue the pieces together. A change in a business process can cause havoc if the set of dependencies is not correctly tracked or accurately represented in some visual model. The impact downstream is particularly significant if the change affects the data model or breaks existing interfaces, and the existing long-running, stateful transactions must successfully complete under the old version of the process.

This example may appear extreme, but highly integrated solutions are now mainstream. This is evident in the choice of integration standards, frameworks, and patterns available. Understanding the implications of change in these outlying systems is critical in ensuring a sustainable level of support to your customers.

Luckily, there are many tools and techniques to mitigate the impact of change:

- Make small, incremental changes
- Build repeatable test cases and run them often
- Make building test cases easier
- Track dependencies
- Act and react systematically
- Automate repetitive tasks

The architect must estimate the effect of change on various aspects of the project's scope, time, and budget, and be prepared to spend more time on those areas whose impact would be the greatest as a result of "a bump in the road." Measuring risk is a useful tool for knowing where your valuable time should be spent.

Reducing complexity is important, but reduced complexity does not equate to simplicity. The payoff for understanding the type and impact of change on your solutions is immeasurable in the medium- to long-term.

Doug Crawford manages a team of middleware developers for a telecommunications company in South Africa. He spent the last 10 years fitting square pegs into round holes, and has been intimately involved on application integration projects in a range of industries: advertising, corporate banking, insurance, and education.

You Have to Understand Hardware, Too

Kamal Wickramanayake

FOR MANY SOFTWARE ARCHITECTS, hardware capacity planning is a topic that lies beyond their comfort zone, yet it remains an important part of the architect's job. There are a number of reasons why software architects often fail to properly consider hardware, but they mostly have to do with a lack of understanding and unclear requirements.

The primary reason we neglect hardware considerations is that we are focused on software and tend to ignore hardware demands. In addition, we are naturally isolated from hardware by high-level languages and software frameworks.

Unclear requirements are also a factor, as they may change or may be poorly understood. As the architecture evolves, hardware considerations will also change. In addition, our clients may not understand or be able to predict the size of their own user base or system usage dynamics. Finally, hardware is constantly evolving. What we knew about hardware in the past does not apply today.

Without hardware expertise, predicting hardware configurations for systems to be developed is highly error prone. To compensate, some software architects use large safety factors. Such safety factors are generally not based on objective assessments or founded in any methodology. In most of the cases, this leads to excessive infrastructure capacities that will not be utilized even in periods of peak demand. As a result, clients' money is wasted on more hardware than a system will ever need.

The best defense against poor hardware planning is to work closely with an infrastructure architect. Infrastructure architects, unlike software architects, are specialists in hardware capacity planning, and they should be a part of your team. However, not every software architect has the luxury of working with an infrastructure architect. In such cases there are some things a software architect can do to mitigate errors when planning for hardware.

Drawing on your own past experience can help. You've implemented systems in the past, so you have some knowledge of hardware capacity planning—even if it was an afterthought at the time. You can also discuss the topic with your client and convince them to set aside funds for hardware capacity planning. Budgeting for capacity planning can be much more cost effective than buying more hardware than you need. In this case, horizontal scalability is the key—adding hardware as needed rather than overbuying in the beginning. To make a horizontal strategy work, software architects need to constantly measure capacity and isolate software components to execute in performance-predictable environments.

Hardware capacity planning is as important as software architecture, and it needs to be given a first-order priority whether you have an infrastructure architect on hand or not. Just as an architect is responsible for establishing the links between business demands and a software solution, she is responsible for envisioning the links between hardware and software.

Kamal Wickramanayake is an IT and software architect who lives in Sri Lanka. He is TOGAF-certified by The Open Group.

Shortcuts Now Are Paid Back with Interest Later

Scot Mcphee

IT'S IMPORTANT TO REMEMBER when architecting a system that maintenance will, in the long run, consume more resources than initial development of the project. Shortcuts taken during the initial development phase of a project can result in significant maintenance costs later.

For example, you may have been informed that unit tests don't deliver direct value, and so you tell your developers to skip the rigorous application of them. This makes the delivered system much more difficult to change in the future, and decreases confidence when making those changes. The system will require far more manual testing for a smaller set of changes, leading to brittleness and increased maintenance expenses as well as a design that's not as appropriate as a fully tested design (let alone a test-first design).

A serious architectural mistake is to adapt an existing system for a purpose that it is not fit for, on the basis that using an existing system somehow reduces costs. For example, you might find yourself utilizing BPEL architectural components coupled with database triggers to deliver an asynchronous messaging system. This might be done or insisted upon for reasons of convenience or because that is the architecture known to you or the client. But a messaging architecture should have been selected in the first instance after requirements made it clear, it was a necessary component. Poor decisions made at the inception of a project make it much more expensive to re-architect the system to meet new requirements.

In addition to avoiding shortcuts during the initial development phase, it's also important to correct poor design decisions as quickly as they are discovered. Poorly designed features can become the foundation for future features, making corrective action later even more costly.

For example, if you discover that inappropriate libraries were selected for some underlying functionality, they should be replaced as soon as possible. Otherwise, the effort to make them fit evolving requirements will result in additional layers of abstractions, each designed to hide the poor fit of the previous layer. You are building yourself a ball of tangled twine, tack, and sticky tape and with every layer you add, it is harder to unravel. This results in a system that is resistant to change.

As an architect, whenever you encounter an architectural problem or design flaw, insist that it be rectified now, when it is cheapest to fix. The longer you leave it to drag out, the higher the interest payment is.

Scot Mcphee is an Australian software developer and architect with more than 15 years of experience coding and designing applications. Over the last eight years, he's worked mostly within the J2EE stack.

"Perfect" Is the Enemy of "Good Enough"

Greg Nyberg

SOFTWARE DESIGNERS, and architects in particular, tend to evaluate solutions by how elegant and optimum they are for a given problem. Like judges at a beauty contest, we look at a design or implementation and immediately see minor flaws or warts that could be eliminated with just a few more changes or refactoring iterations. Domain models simply beg for one more pass to see if there are any common attributes or functions that can be moved into base classes. Services duplicated in multiple implementations cry out their need to become web services. Queries complain about "buffer gets" and nonunique indexes, and demand attention.

My advice: don't give in to the temptation to make your design, or your implementation, perfect! Aim for "good enough" and stop when you've achieved it.

What exactly is "good enough," you might ask? Good enough means that the remaining imperfections do not impact system functionality, maintainability, or performance in any meaningful way. The architecture and design hangs together. The implementation works and meets the performance requirements. Code is clear, concise, and well documented. Could it be better? Sure, but it is good enough, so stop. Declare victory and move on to the next task.

The search for perfection in design and implementation leads, in my opinion, to overdesigned and obfuscated solutions that are, in the end, harder to maintain.

A number of the axioms in this book caution designers to avoid unnecessary abstraction or complexity. Why do we have problems keeping things simple? Because we are seeking the perfect solution! Why else would an architect introduce complexity in a workable solution except to address a perceived imperfection in the simpler design?

Remember that application development is not a beauty contest, so stop looking for flaws and wasting time chasing perfection.

> *Greg Nyberg is currently an independent J2EE computer consultant with 18 years' experience designing, building, testing, and deploying large, high-volume, transactional applications such as reservation systems, call centers, and consumer websites. He is the author of the WebLogic companion workbook for* Enterprise JavaBeans, *Third Edition, (O'Reilly), and the lead author of the book* Mastering WebLogic Server *(Wiley).*

Avoid "Good Ideas"

Greg Nyberg

GOOD IDEAS KILL PROJECTS. Sometimes it's a quick death, but often it's a slow, lingering death caused by missed milestones and a spiraling bug count.

You know the kinds of good ideas I'm talking about: tempting, no-brainer, innocent-looking, couldn't-possibly-hurt-to-try sorts of ideas. They usually occur to someone on the team about halfway through a project when every-thing seems to be going fine. Stories and tasks are getting knocked off at a good pace, initial testing is going well, and the rollout date looks solid. Life is good.

Someone has a "good idea," you acquiesce, and suddenly you are refitting a new version of Hibernate into your project to take advantage of the latest fea-tures, or implementing AJAX in some of your web pages because the devel-oper showed the user how cool it is, or even revisiting the database design to utilize XML features of the RDBMS. You tell the project manager you need a few weeks to implement this "good idea," but it ends up impacting more code than originally anticipated, and your schedule starts to slip. Plus, by letting in the first "good idea," you've allowed the proverbial camel's nose in the tent, and soon the good ideas are coming out of the woodwork and it becomes harder to say no (and the camel is soon sleeping in your bed).

The really insidious thing about "good ideas" is that they are "good." Every-one can recognize and reject "bad" ideas out of hand—it's the good ones that slip through and cause trouble with scope, complexity, and sheer wasted effort incorporating something into the application that isn't necessary to meet the business need.

Here are some key phrases to look for:

- "Wouldn't it be cool if…." Really, any sentence with the word "cool" in it is a danger signal.

- "Hey, they just released version XXX of the YYY framework. We ought to upgrade!"

- "You know, we really should refactor XXX as long as we are working on ZZZ…."

- "That XXX technology is really powerful! Maybe we could use it on…."

- "Hey, <*yournamehere*>, I've been thinking about the design and I have an idea!"

OK, OK, maybe I'm being a bit too cynical with that last one. But keep watching out for "good ideas" that can kill your project.

Author bio available on page 141.

Great Content Creates Great Systems

Zubin Wadia

I HAVE SEEN MY FAIR SHARE of initiatives focus endlessly on requirements, design, development, security, and maintenance, but not on the actual point of the system—the data. This is especially true in content-based systems in which the data is information delivered as unstructured or semi-structured content. Great content means the difference between a system that is hollow and one that is relevant.

Content is king. Content is the network. Content is the interface. In an increasingly interconnected world, content quality is rapidly becoming the difference between success and failure. FaceBook versus Orkut/Google versus Cuil/NetFlix versus BlockbusterOnline...the list is endless where battles have been won and lost on the content battlefield. One could argue that content-related aspects are not the software architect's problem—but I think the next decade will certainly disprove that.

Part of the design process for a new system should be devoted to assessing content inventory. Designing an effective domain/object/data model is not enough.

Analyze all available content and assess its value on the following criteria:

- Is there enough content available? If not, how do we attain critical mass?

- Is the content fresh enough? If not, how do we improve delivery rates?

- Have all possible content channels been explored? RSS feeds, email, and paper forms are all channels.

- Are there effective input streams built to facilitate the continual delivery of this content into the system? It's one thing to identify valuable content, but another thing altogether to harvest it regularly.

Make no mistake, the success of a system depends on its content. Spend a healthy part of the design process to assess the value of your content. If your findings are less than satisfactory, then that's a red flag the stakeholders must be advised about. I have seen many systems that fulfill all contractual obligations, meet every requirement, and still fail because this fairly obvious aspect was ignored. Great content creates great systems.

> *Zubin Wadia is CEO at RedRock IT Solutions and CTO at ImageWork Technologies. He has a diverse software programming background with knowledge of Basic, C, C++, Perl, Java, JSP, JSF, JavaScript, Erlang, Scala, Eiffel, and Ruby languages. His main focus is on enabling Fortune Global 500 companies and U.S. government agencies through business process-automation solutions.*

The Business Versus the Angry Architect

Chad LaVigne

THERE COMES A TIME IN OUR CAREERS as architects when we realize many of the issues we encounter are recurring. Though the project and industry may change, many of the problems are similar. At this point we can draw on our experience to provide many solutions quickly, leaving more time to enjoy the challenging issues. We're confident in our solutions and we deliver as advertised. We have reached homeostasis. This is the perfect time to make a colossal mistake—like deciding you know so much that it's time for you to start talking more than you listen. This poor decision usually comes with a side of cynicism, impatience, and general anger toward inferior minds who dare contradict your superior understanding of all things technical and otherwise.

In its worst form this overconfidence bleeds into the business realm. This is an excellent way to land your career on a list somewhere next to the Black Rhino. The business is our reason for existence. That statement probably hurts a little, but we must not lose sight of that fact. We live to serve them, not vice versa. Listening to and understanding the business that employs us to solve problems is the most critical skill we possess. Ever caught yourself impatiently waiting for a business analyst to finish talking so you could make your point? Chances are, you didn't get his. Show the business domain experts the respect you expect to receive; this is the last group of people you want viewing you as unapproachable. If they start avoiding you, you're being a catalyst for communication breakdown and sabotaging your own project. Remember, when you're talking you can only hear something you already know. Don't ever start thinking you're so smart that no one else has something valuable to say.

When we are listening, we'll often disagree with what we hear about how the business operates. That's fine. We can make suggestions for improvement and should definitely do so. However, if at the end of the day you disagree with how the business is run and it's not going to change, that's just too bad. Don't allow yourself to become a disgruntled genius who spends all of his time trying to impress others by making witty, condescending statements about how poorly the company is run. They won't be impressed. They've met that guy before and they don't really like him. One of the key ingredients to the recipe for a great architect is passion for your work, but you don't want too much passion of the angry variety. Learn to accept disagreements and move on. If the differences are too great and you find yourself continually at odds with the business, find a company that's easier for you to get behind and design solutions for them. Regardless of how, find a way to establish a good relationship with the business and don't let your ego damage it. It will make you a happier, more productive architect.

Author bio available on page 111.

Stretch Key Dimensions to See What Breaks

Stephen Jones

AN APPLICATION'S DESIGN IS OUTLINED initially based on the specified business requirements, selected or existing technologies, performance envelope, expected data volumes, and the financial resources available to build, deploy, and operate it. The solution, whatever it is, will meet or exceed what is asked of it in the contemporary environment and is expected to run successfully (or it is not yet a solution).

Now take this solution and stretch the key dimensions to see what breaks.

This examination looks for limits in the design that will occur when, for example, the system becomes wildly popular and more customers use it, the products being processed increase their transaction counts per day, or six months of data must now be retained rather than the initially specified week. Dimensions are stretched individually and then in combination to tease out the unseen limits that might lie hidden in the initial design.

Stretching key dimensions allows an architect to validate a solution by:

- Understanding whether the planned infrastructure accommodates these increases, and where the limits are. If the infrastructure will break, this process identifies where it will break, which can be highlighted for the application's owner, or the planned infrastructure can be purchased with specific upgrade paths in mind.

- Confirming that there are sufficient hours in the day to perform the processing at the expected throughput, with head room to accommodate "busy days" or "catch up" after an outage. A solution that cannot complete a day's processing in a day and relies on the weekend when things are quieter has no long-term future.

- Validating that the data access choices that were made are still valid as the system scales. What might work for a week's worth of data may be unusable with six month's data loaded.

- Confirming how the application's increased workload will be scaled across additional hardware (if required), and the transition path as the load increases. Working through the transition before the application is deployed can influence the data stored and its structure.

- Confirming that the application can still be recovered if the data volumes are increased and/or the data is now split among an increased infrastructure.

Based on this examination, elements of the design may be recognised as problems requiring redesign. The redesign will be cheaper whilst the design is still virtual, technical choices are not locked-in and the business data has yet to be stored in the repositories.

Stephen Jones designs solutions for Tier-1 Telco Billing and its related high-volume processes for companies such as Telstra and Optus in Australia, and the 1997 version of AT&T in the U.S. This design work included the initial implementations of Telco billing systems, redesigns of post-bill dispute and fraud billing functions, and over two years managing 24/7 production support for Telstra.

If You Design It, You Should Be Able to Code It

Mike Brown

IN ARCHITECTURE, it's tempting to create elaborate designs and abstractions that elegantly address the problem at hand. It is even more tempting to sprinkle new technologies into the project. At the end of the day, someone has to implement your design, and the architectural acrobatics that you have the developers perform impact the project.

When designing the architecture for your project, you need to have a feel for the amount of effort necessary to implement each element of your design; if you've developed an element before, it will be much easier to estimate the effort required.

Don't use a pattern in your design that you haven't personally implemented before. Don't rely on a framework that you haven't coded against before. Don't use a server that you haven't configured before. If your architecture depends on design elements that you haven't personally used, there are a number of negative side effects:

- You will not have experienced the learning curve that your developers will have to face. If you don't know how long it takes to learn a new technology, you won't be able to give a good estimate on time to implement.

- You will not know the pitfalls to avoid when using the elements. Inevitably, things will not go as well as the demo that the trained expert in the technology provided. If you haven't worked with the technology before, you will be blindsided when this happens.

- You will lose the confidence of your developers. When they ask questions about the design and you aren't able to give solid answers, they will quickly lose confidence in you and your design.

- You will introduce unnecessary risk. Not knowing these things can put a big question mark on key elements of the solution. No one wants to start a project with big, unnecessary risks hanging around.

So how does one go about learning new frameworks, patterns, and server platforms? Well, that's another axiom in and of itself: before anything, an architect is a developer.

Author bio available on page 127.

A Rose by Any Other Name Will End Up As a Cabbage

Sam Gardiner

I OVERHEARD SOME PEOPLE DECIDING that they need more layers in their architecture. They were right, as it happens, but going about it a little backward. They were attempting to create a framework that would contain the business logic. Rather than solving some specific problems they started with the idea that they want a framework that wraps the database up and produces objects. And it should use object-relational mapping. And messages. And web services. And it should do all sorts of cool stuff.

Unfortunately, since they didn't exactly know what cool stuff it would do, they didn't know what to call it. So they held a little competition to suggest a name. And that is the point at which you must recognise that you have a problem: if you don't know what a thing should be called, you cannot know what it is. If you don't know what it is, you cannot sit down and write the code.

In this particular case, a quick browse throughout the source control history revealed the depth of the problem. Of course, there were lots of empty interface "implementations"! And the really funny thing is that they had already changed the names three times with no actual code. When they started they called it ClientAPI—the "client" refers to the customers of the business, not client as in "client-server"—and the final version was called ClientBusinessObjects. Great name: vague, broad, and misleading.

Of course, in the end, a name is just a pointer. Once everyone involved knows that the name is just a name and not a design metaphor then you can all move on. However, if you can't agree on a name that is specific enough for you to know when it is wrong, then you might have some difficulty even getting started. Design is all about trying to fulfill intentions—e.g., fast, cheap, flexible—and names convey intentions.

If you can't name it, you can't write it. If you change the name three times, then you should stop until you know what you are trying to build.

After a lifetime of playing with computers—starting with writing games in BASIC on the BBC computer and going on to such diverse elements as pascal, Mathematica, and using Labview to process hand-rolled databases made of raw text data files from experiments held together with sticky tape—Sam Gardiner stumbled into professional software development. He has been working in the software industry for six years.

Stable Problems Get High-Quality Solutions

Sam Gardiner

REAL-WORLD PROGRAMMING is not about solving the problem that some-one gives to you. In the computer science classroom, you must solve the binary-sort problem given to you. In the real world, the best architects don't solve hard problems, they work around them. The skill is in drawing boundar-ies around diffuse and diverse software problems so that they are stable and self-contained.

An architect should be able to look at a whole mess of concepts and data and process and separate them into smaller pieces or "chunks." The important thing about those problem chunks is that they are stable, allowing them to be solved by a system chunk that is finite and stable in scope. The problem chunks should be:

- Internally cohesive: the chunk is conceptually unified, so all of the tasks, data, and features are related

- Well separated from other chunks: the chunks are conceptually normal-ized; there is little or no overlap between them

The person who is excessively good at doing this may not even know that she is doing it, just as a person with a good sense of direction knows where she is. It just seems to make sense to her to break up the tasks, data, and features in a way that provides a nice edge or interface to the system. I'm not talking about the actual interfaces of an object-oriented language, but system boundaries.

For instance, a relational database management system has a very nice system boundary. It manages literally any type of data that can be serialized into a stream of bytes, and it can organize, search, and retrieve that data. Simple.

What is interesting is that if the problem is stable, then when it is solved, it is solved permanently. In five/fifty years' time you might want to slap a web/ telepathic interface over it, but your core system won't need to change. The system is durable because the problem is durable.

Of course, the code needs to be pretty neat, but if the problem is neat, the code can be neat, as there are no special cases. And neat code is good because it is easy to test and easy to review, and that means that the implementation quality can be very high. As you don't have messy code, you can concentrate on things that are outside the domain of user-visible features like using reliable messaging or distributed transactions, or driving up performance by using multithreading or even low-level languages like assembly code. Because the problem isn't changing, you can concentrate on driving up the quality to the point where it is a feature.

A stable problem allows you to create a system with a stable design; stable design allows you to concentrate on making an application that has very high quality.

Author bio available on page 153.

It Takes Diligence

Brian Hart

AN ARCHITECT'S JOB IS OFTEN PORTRAYED as an activity focused on ingenuity and problem solving. Ingenuity is a key trait of successful architects. However, an equally important characteristic of the activities of a successful architect is diligence. Diligence can manifest itself in many ways, but ultimately it is an exercise in perseverance and paying the right amount of attention to each task and each architectural goal of the system.

Diligence goes hand in hand with the mundane. Successful architecture practices are in many ways mundane. Effective architects often follow mundane daily and weekly checklists to remind them of that which they already know academically, but fail to practice by habit. Without such mundane checklists and reminders, architects can quickly fall into software time, in which no measurable progress is achieved because a lack of diligence allowed the architecture to meander and violate known academic principles. It is important to realize in these retrospectives of failed projects that in most cases it isn't incompetence that drove failure, but rather the lack of both diligence and a sense of urgency.

Diligence also requires an architect to succeed at the deceptively simple task of making and keeping commitments. These commitments are often disparate and can encompass a wide range of constraints and expectations. Examples include:

- Embracing the budget and time constraints of the customer

- Performing all the work that makes the architect effective, not just the work the architect enjoys

- Committing to the process/methodology

- Accepting responsibility

Atul Gawande, in his terrific book *Better: A Surgeon's Notes on Performance* (Metropolitan Books), speaks of diligence in the medical community:

> True success in medicine is not easy. It requires will, attention to detail, and creativity. But the lesson I took from India was that it is possible anywhere and by anyone. I can imagine few places with more difficult conditions. Yet astonishing success could be found... what I saw was: Better is possible. It does not take genius. It takes diligence. It takes moral clarity. It takes ingenuity. And above all, it takes a willingness to try.

Brian Hart is an executive consultant with CGI, a leading IT and business process services provider. Brian is involved in the architecture and design of J2EE applications primarily in the state and local government sector. He has been involved in the software industry since 1997.

Take Responsibility for Your Decisions

Yi Zhou

SOFTWARE ARCHITECTS HAVE TO TAKE RESPONSIBILITY for their decisions, as they have much more influential power in software projects than most people in organizations. Studies of software projects show that more than two-thirds of them either are outright failures or deliver unsuccessfully (deadline slip, budget overruns, or low customer satisfaction). Many of the root causes point to improper decisions software architects made, or failures of follow-through on the right architectural decisions.

How can you become a responsible software architect who makes effective architectural decisions?

First, you have to be fully cognizant of your decision process, whether it is agile or ceremonial. You should *not* claim that an architectural decision has been made until the following two conditions are met:

- A decision has been put in writing because architectural decisions are rarely trivial. They must be substantiated and traceable.

- A decision has been communicated to the people who execute it and the people who will be affected directly or indirectly. Communication is all about creating shared understanding.

Second, review your architectural decisions periodically. Examine the results of your decisions against expectations. Identify architectural decisions that remain valid and those that do not.

Third, enforce your architectural decisions. Many software projects get software architects involved only in the design phase, then they move on to other projects or the consultation contract ends. How can they ensure that their deliberate architectural decisions have been implemented correctly? Their decisions will be at best good intentions unless they follow through with them.

Finally, delegate some decision making to others who are experts in a problem domain. Many architects wrongly assume they have to make every architectural decision. Therefore, they position themselves as know-it-all experts. In reality, there's no such thing as a universal technical genius. Architects have areas in which they are quite proficient, areas in which they are knowledgeable, and areas in which they are simply incompetent. Adept architects delegate decisions about domain problems in which they are not proficient.

> *Yi Zhou is currently the chief software architect in a well-known biotech company, and specializes in designing the software platform for medical devices and personalizing disease management. He has nearly 20 years' experience in all aspects of the software development life cycle, and excels in business-technology alignment and strategic planning, process improvement, architecture and framework design, team building and management, and consulting.*

Don't Be Clever

Eben Hewitt

GENERAL INTELLIGENCE, RESOURCEFULNESS, thoughtfulness, a breadth and depth of knowledge, and an affinity for precision are laudable qualities in anyone, and particularly prized in architects.

Cleverness, however, carries a certain additional connotation. It implies an ability to quickly conceive of a solution that may get you out of a jam, but that ultimately rests on a gimmick, a shell game, or a switcharoo. We remember clever debaters from high school—always able to play semantics or work the logical fallacies to win the point.

Clever software is expensive, hard to maintain, and brittle. Don't be clever. Be as dumb as you possibly can and still create the appropriate design. The appropriate design will never be clever. If cleverness appears absolutely required, the problem is incorrectly framed; reset the problem. Reframe it until you can be dumb again. Work in rough chalk sketches; stay general. Let go of the flavor of the day. It takes a smart architect to be dumb.

It is our cleverness that allows us to trick software into working. Don't be the attorney who gets your software off on a technicality. We are not Rube Goldberg. We are not MacGyver, ever ready to pull some complicated design out of our hats having been allowed only a paper clip, a firecracker, and a piece of chewing gum. Empty your head and approach the problem without your extensive knowledge of closures and generics and how to manipulate object graduation in the heap. Sometimes of course, such stuff is exactly what we need. But less often than we might think.

More developers can implement and maintain dumb solutions. In dumb solutions, each component can do only one thing. They will take less time to create, and less time to change later. They inherit optimizations from the building blocks you're using. They emerge from the page as a living process, and you can feel their elegance and simplicity. Clever designs will stay stubbornly rooted; their details are too embroiled in the overall picture. They crumble if you touch them.

> *Eben Hewitt is a principal on the architecture team at a multibillion-dollar national retail company, where he is currently focused on designing and implementing its service-oriented architecture. He is the author of the upcoming* Java SOA Cookbook *from O'Reilly.*

Choose Your Weapons Carefully, Relinquish Them Reluctantly

Chad LaVigne

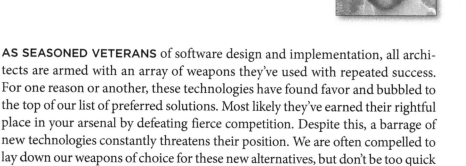

AS SEASONED VETERANS of software design and implementation, all architects are armed with an array of weapons they've used with repeated success. For one reason or another, these technologies have found favor and bubbled to the top of our list of preferred solutions. Most likely they've earned their rightful place in your arsenal by defeating fierce competition. Despite this, a barrage of new technologies constantly threatens their position. We are often compelled to lay down our weapons of choice for these new alternatives, but don't be too quick to dismiss your trusty armaments. To cast them aside for alternatives that haven't been proven through similar trials is a risky proposition.

This doesn't mean that, once established on our list of favorites, a technology is granted infinite tenure and it certainly doesn't mean that you can bury your head in the sand and ignore advancements in software development. For each technology, a time will come when it needs to be replaced. Technology moves quickly, and superior solutions are on the way. As architects we need to stay abreast of industry trends, but we don't need to be the first to embrace fledgling technology. There's usually no huge advantage to being the first to adopt new technology, but there can be several drawbacks.

To justify the risk involved with selecting new technology, its benefits should be a quantum leap forward. Many new technologies claim such advancement, but few deliver it. It's easy to look at new technology and see technical advantages, but those benefits are often difficult to sell to stakeholders. Before you decide to blaze a trail with new technology, ask yourself how the business will benefit from this decision. If the best outcome from a business perspective is that no one will notice, rethink your decision.

Another important thing to acknowledge is the cost associated with the shortcomings of new technology. These costs can be high and are difficult to calculate. When you're working with familiar technology you're aware of its idiosyncrasies. It's naïve to think that a new technology won't come with its own collection of pitfalls. Adding problems that you haven't solved before will destroy your estimates. You're far more aware of the costs involved when implementing solutions using familiar technology.

One last thing to consider is future relevance. It would be nice if we could simply identify and select superior technologies, but things aren't quite that simple. Great technologies don't always win. Trying to predict the winners early is a gamble that doesn't yield a large payoff. Wait for the hype to die down and see if the technology settles into a space of usefulness. You'll find that many just go away. Don't jeopardize your project for a technology that doesn't have a future.

Selecting the technologies we use to attack problems is a large part of the software architect's job. Choose your weapons carefully and relinquish them reluctantly. Let your past success help to ensure future success, and evolve your technology stack cautiously.

Author bio available on page 111.

Your Customer Is Not Your Customer

Eben Hewitt

AS YOU WORK IN REQUIREMENTS MEETINGS to design software, pretend that your customer is not your customer. It turns out that this is a very easy thing to do, because it is true.

Your customer is not your customer. Your customer's customer is your customer. If your customer's customer wins, your customer wins. Which means you win.

If you're writing an e-commerce application, take care of the things that you know people who will shop at that site will need. They'll need transport security. They'll need encryption of stored data. Your customer may not mention these requirements. If you know that your customer is leaving out things your customer's customer will need, address them, and communicate why.

If your customer willingly and knowingly doesn't care about certain important things that your customer's customer cares about—as happens from time to time—consider stepping away from the project. Just because Sally Customer doesn't want to pay for SSL every year and wants to store credit cards in plain text because it costs less to build, it's not OK to simply agree. You're killing your customer's customer when you agree to do work you know is a bad idea.

Requirements-gathering meetings are not implementation meetings. Forbid the customer's use of implementation-specific terms unless it's an absolute or well-understood problem. Allow your customer to express only the Platonic ideal, his concept and goals, rather than dictating a solution or even using technical terms.

So, how do you maintain such discipline in these meetings, which can be deceptively difficult? Remember to care for your customer's customer. Remember that while your customer is writing your check, you must be clear that you need to honor best practices, so that you can make what the customer really needs, not just what they say they need. Of course, this takes lots of discussion, and clarity as to exactly what you're doing and why.

Perhaps, as with so many things in life, this is best clarified by a poem. In 1649, Richard Lovelace wrote "To Lucasta, on Going to the Wars." It ends with the line: "I could not love thee, dear, so much,/Loved I not honor more."

We cannot love our customers so much, love we not their customers more.

Author bio available on page 161.

It Will Never
Look Like That

Peter Gillard-Moss

IT WILL NEVER LOOK LIKE THAT. It is all too easy to fall into the trap of investing large amounts of time in a design and being confident that the implementation will come out the same. A detailed design can easily fool you into believing you have every angle covered. The greater the detail and the more in-depth the research, the greater your confidence in it. But it is an illusion: it will never look like that.

The truth is, no matter how in-depth, how well researched, and how well thought-out your design, it will never come out looking the same as in your head. Something will happen, an external factor may affect the design: incorrect information, a limitation, an odd behaviour in someone else's code. Or you may have got something wrong: an oversight, an incorrect presumption, a subtle concept missed. Or something will change: the requirements, the technology, or someone may just find a better way™.

Those minor alterations in the design soon stack up and lots of minor alterations soon require that one big one has to be made. Before long your original concept is on the floor in pieces, and it's back to the drawing board. You decide what you needed was more design and more detail, so back you go, and the next architectural vision is clearer, more radical, more perfect than the last.

But before long the same thing happens. Those changes start to appear and shift your design, and developers keep shoving in more and more stuff trying their best to work around the broken design but just breaking it more, and you end up screaming, "Of course it's got bugs; it was never designed to do that!"

Design is a discovery process; as we implement, we discover new information that is often impossible to know upfront. By accepting that design is an ongoing and empirical process in a forever-changing world, we learn that the design process must be flexible and ongoing, too. Clinging to your original designs and trying to force them through is only going to produce one result, so you need to understand that *it will never look like that*.

Peter Gillard-Moss is a ThoughtWorker and general memeologist living in the U.K. He has worked in IT since 2000 on many projects, from public-facing websites in media and e-commerce to rich-client banking applications and corporate intranets.

Choose Frameworks That Play Well with Others

Eric Hawthorne

WHEN CHOOSING SOFTWARE FRAMEWORKS as a basis of your system, you must consider not only the individual quality and features of each framework, but also how well the set of frameworks that make up your system will work together, and how easy it will be to adapt them to new software you may need to add as your system evolves. This means you must choose frameworks that do not overlap and that are humble, simple, and specialized.

It is best if each framework or third-party library addresses a separate logical domain or concern, and does not tread into the domain or concern of another framework you need to use.

Make sure you understand how the logical domains and concerns addressed by your candidate frameworks overlap. Draw a Venn diagram if you need to. Two data models that overlap substantially in domain, or two implementations that address very similar concerns but in slightly different ways, will cause unnecessary complexity: the slight differences in conceptualization or representation must be mapped or patched with kludgy glue code. Chances are, you'll end up not only with complex glue, but also with the lowest-common-denominator of the functionality or representative power of the two frameworks.

To minimize the chance that any given framework will overlap with another framework, choose frameworks that have a high utility-to-baggage ratio, in the context of your system requirements. Utility is the functionality or data representation that your project needs from the framework. Baggage is the framework's sweeping, all-encompassing, I'm-in-charge view of the world. Does it insist on mixing data representation and control? Does its data model or set of packages and classes extend well beyond what your system needs? Do you have to become a fundamentalist in the framework's religion, and limit your choices of other frameworks to those of the correct denomination? Does its excess complexity limit the kinds of things you can mix with it? If a framework comes with lots of baggage, then that it had also better be providing 75% of the functionality value in your project.

Your system should be comprised of mutually exclusive frameworks, each of which may be a master of its domain, but which is also simple, humble, and flexible.

Eric Hawthorne has architected, designed, and developed object-oriented software and distributed systems professionally since 1988, beginning and for 10 years at Macdonald Dettwiler, a Canadian systems-engineering company, where among other things, he had the opportunity to absorb some architectural technique from Philippe Kruchten.

Make a Strong Business Case

Yi Zhou

AS A SOFTWARE ARCHITECT, have you had a hard time getting your architecture project well funded? The benefits of software architecture are obvious for architects, but are mythical for many stakeholders. Mass psychology tells us that "seeing is believing" is the strongest belief for most people. At the early phase of the projects, however, there is little to demonstrate to convince stakeholders of the value of sound software architecture. It's even more challenging in the nonsoftware industries where most stakeholders have little software-engineering knowledge.

Mass psychology also shows that most people believe in "perception is reality." Therefore, if you can control how people perceive the architectural approach you propose, it's virtually guaranteed that you can control how they will react to your proposal. How can you mange stakeholders' perceptions? Make a strong business case for your architecture. People who have the budget authority to sponsor your ideas are almost always business-driven.

I have employed the following five steps to generate solid business cases to successfully sell my architectural approach many times in my career:

1. *Establish the value proposition.* The value proposition is your executive summary of why your organization's business warrants a particular software architecture. The key for this is to compare your architectural approach with existing solutions or other alternatives. The focus should be put on its capability to increase the productivity and efficiency of the business rather than how brilliant the technologies are.

2. *Build metrics to quantify.* The values you promise to deliver need to be quantified to a reasonable extent. The more you measure, the more you can bolster your case that sound architecture will lead to a substantial return. The earlier you establish metrics, the better you manage people's perceptions that help you sell responsible architecture.

3. *Link back to traditional business measures.* It would be ideal if you can translate your technical analysis into dollar figures. After all, the only constant parameter in the traditional business measures is money. Find business analysts as your partners if you are not comfortable with financial work.

4. *Know where to stop.* Before you know where to stop, you need to prepare a roadmap that captures a vision with each milestone on it tied directly to business values. Let the stakeholders decide where to stop. If the business value for each momentum is significant, you're most likely to get continued funding.

5. *Find the right timing.* Even if you follow the previous four steps to generate a solid business case, you still may not be able to sell your ideas if you pick the bad timing. I remember one of my proposals did not get approved for a long time until another project turned out to be a total failure because of poor architectural design. Be smart on timing.

Author bio available on page 159.

Control the Data,
Not Just the Code

Chad LaVigne

SOURCE CODE CONTROL AND CONTINUOUS INTEGRATION are excellent tools for managing the application build and deployment process. Along with source code, schema and data changes are often a significant part of this process and thus warrant similar controls. If your build and deployment process includes a list of elaborate steps required for data updates, beware. These are the lists that always have you crossing your fingers. They look something like this:

1. Create a list of scripts that need to be run, in order.

2. E-mail scripts to special database person.

3. Database person copies the scripts to a location where they're executed by a cron job.

4. Check script execution log and pray that all scripts ran successfully since you're not exactly sure what will happen if you rerun them.

5. Run validation scripts and spot-check the data.

6. Regression test the application and see what blows up.

7. Write scripts to insert missing data and fix blow-ups.

8. Repeat.

OK, so that might be a slight exaggeration but it's not that far off. Many a project requires this type of acrobatic workflow for successful database migration.

For some reason the data portion of the migration plan seems to be easily overlooked during architecture planning. As a result, it can become a brittle, manual process that gets bolted on as an afterthought.

This complex web-work creates many opportunities for process breakdown. To make matters worse, bugs caused by schema and data changes don't always get caught by unit tests as part of the nightly build report. They like to rear their ugly head in a loud, boisterous manner immediately after a build has been migrated. Database problems are usually tedious to reverse by hand and their solutions tend to be more difficult to validate. The value of a completely automated build process that is capable of restoring the database to a known state will never be more evident than when you're using it to fix an extremely visible issue. If you don't have the ability to drop the database and restore it to a state that is compatible with a specific build of the application, you are susceptible to the same type of problems you'd have if you couldn't back out a code change quickly.

Database changes shouldn't create a ripple in your build's time-space continuum. You need to be able to build the entire application, including the database, as one unit. Make data and schema management a seamless part of your automated build and testing process early on and include an undo button; it will pay large dividends. At best it will save hours of painful, high-stress problem solving after a late night blunder. At worst it will give your team the ability to confidently charge forward with refactoring of the data access layer.

Author bio available on page 111.

Pay Down Your Technical Debt

Burkhardt Hufnagel

ON ANY PROJECT THAT IS IN PRODUCTION (i.e., it has customers that are using it), there will come a time when a change must be made; either a bug needs fixing, or a new feature must be added. At that point there are two possible choices: you can take the time needed to "do it right," or you can take one or more "shortcuts" and try to get the change out the door sooner.

Generally, the business people (sales/marketing and customers) will want the change made as quickly as possible, while the developers and testers will be more interested in taking the time to properly design, implement, and test the change before delivering it to the customers.

As the project's architect, you'll have to decide which makes more sense and then convince the decision makers to take your advice; and, as with most architectural issues, there is a tradeoff involved. If you believe the system is reasonably stable, then it may make sense to go the "quick and dirty" route and get the change into production quickly. That's fine, but you need to know that in doing so your project is incurring some "technical debt" that must be repaid later. Repayment, in this case, means going back and making the change in the way you would have if you'd had the time and resources to do it right the first time.

So why the concern over making changes properly now versus later? It's because there's a hidden cost to making these quick and dirty fixes. For financial debts the hidden cost is called "interest," and most anyone with a credit card knows how expensive just paying the interest on a debt can be. For technical debt, interest takes the form of instability in the system, and increased maintenance costs due to the hacked-in changes and lack of proper design, documentation, and/or tests. And, like financial interest, regular payments must be made until the original debt is repaid.

Now that you understand a bit more about the true cost of technical debt, you might decide the price is too high and you can't afford the cost. But when it's a choice between having the developers get the fix out as quickly as possible or taking a severe financial hit, it generally makes sense to get the fix out quickly. So, take the hit and get the change into production ASAP, but don't stop there.

Once the fix is in production, have the developers go back and fix it properly so that it can be included in the next scheduled release. This is the equivalent of charging something on your credit card and then paying off the balance at the end of the month so you don't get charged interest. This way you can provide the fast changes the business needs, while keeping your project out of debtor's prison.

Burk Hufnagel has been creating positive user experiences since 1978 and is a lead software architect at LexisNexis.

Don't Be a Problem Solver

Eben Hewitt

WITH SOME EXCEPTIONS, ARCHITECTS USED TO BE DEVELOPERS. Developers get rewarded for solving programming problems, which are more local in scope than architectural problems. Many programming problems are small, tricky, algorithmic problems. Such problems are frequently presented in programming interviews, books, and university courses as if the problems exist in a vacuum. The trickiness is alluring and seductive. Over time, we begin to accept such problems out of hand. We do not ask if this problem is meaningful, or interesting, or useful, or ethical. We are not rewarded for considering the relation of this problem to a larger landscape. We are trained to focus only on our solution, which is aggravated by the fact that solving hard problems is hard. We leap into action in programming interviews, which often begin by presenting us with some number of jelly beans we are meant to sort according to an arbitrary set of constraints. We learn not to question the constraints; they are a pedagogical tool, intended to lead us to discover what the teacher or interviewer or mentor already knows.

Architects and developers learn to enter problem-solving mode immediately. But sometimes the best solution is no solution. Many software problems need not be solved at all. They only appear as problems because we look only at the symptoms.

Consider managed memory. Developers on managed platforms have not solved memory problems, nor could many of them do so if required; part of their solution means that they mostly just don't have that problem.

Consider complex builds that demand lots of interconnected scripts requiring the enforcement of many standards and conventions. You could solve that problem, and it would feel great to get it all to work, putting your best scripting skills and best practices to work. Our colleagues will be impressed. No one is impressed by us not solving a problem. But if we can step back and figure out that we aren't solving a build problem but rather an automation and portability problem, this might lead you to a tool that abstracts it away.

Because architects tend to immediately enter problem-solving mode, we forget, or rather have never learned how, to interrogate the problem itself. We must learn, like a telephoto lens, to zoom in and zoom out, in order to ensure that the question is really framed properly, and that we're not merely accepting what we're given. We must not be passive receptacles for requirements, cheerfully ready at our posts, handing out our smartest solutions in the manner of a Pez dispenser.

Instead of immediately working to solve the problem as presented, see if you can change the problem. Ask yourself, what would the architecture look like if I just didn't have this problem? This can lead ultimately to more elegant and sustainable solutions. The business problem still does need to be solved, but not, perhaps, as immediately suggested.

We have to break our addiction to "problems." We love to get them, seeing ourselves on a European bridge, as if we are secret agents who've just been handed a self-destructing brown envelope containing our mission. Before considering your answer to a problem, think what the world would look like if you just didn't have this problem.

Author bio available on page 161.

Build Systems to Be Zuhanden

Keith Braithwaite

WE BUILD TOOLS. The systems that we make have no other reason to exist (nor we to get paid) than to help someone, usually someone else, do something.

Martin Heidegger, an influential German philosopher of the 20th century, explored the ways that people experience tools (and more generally "equipment") in their lives. People use tools to work toward a goal, and the tool is merely a means to an end.

During successful use, a tool is *zuhanden* ("ready-to-hand," having the property of "handiness"). The tool is experienced directly; it is used without consideration, without theorisation. We grasp the tool and use it to move toward our goal. In use, it vanishes! The tool becomes an extension of the user's body and is not experienced in its own right. One sign of a tool being zuhanden is that it becomes invisible, unfelt, insignificant.

Consider what it feels like to hammer a nail or to write with a pen. Think about that immediacy. Think about the way the tool seems to be a seamless extension of your body.

Alternatively, and usually when something has gone wrong with it, the user may experience a tool as *vorhanden* ("present-at-hand"). The tool is isolated from the goal; it lies before us demanding attention. It becomes a topic of investigation in its own right. The user is no longer able to proceed toward his goal but must deal first with the tool, without it doing anything to move him toward his goal. As technologists we tend to experience the systems we build for users as vorhanden while we build them, and again when we receive defect reports. For us, the tool is quite properly an object of enquiry, of theorising, of investigation. It is a thing to be studied.

However, it is crucial to their success that the users experience the tools we build for them as zuhanden. Are your systems architected to be invisible in use? Does the user interface fall naturally to hand? Or do your systems keep demanding attention, distracting users from their goal?

Author bio available on page 21.

Find and Retain
Passionate
Problem Solvers

Chad LaVigne

PUTTING TOGETHER A TEAM of outstanding developers is one of the most important things you can do to ensure the success of a software project. While the concept of keeping that team together does not seem to get as much lip service, it is equally important. Therefore, you need to carefully select your development team and diligently protect it once assembled.

Most people probably agree that finding top-notch developers requires thorough technical interviewing. But what does thorough mean exactly? It doesn't mean requiring candidates to answer difficult questions about obscure technical details. Screening for specific technical knowledge is definitely part of the process but turning an interview into a certification test will not guarantee success. You are searching for developers with problem-solving skills and passion. The tools you use are sure to change; you need people who are good at attacking problems regardless of the technologies involved. Proving someone has the ability to recite every method in an API tells you very little about that person's aptitude or passion for solving problems.

However, asking someone to explain her approach to diagnosing a performance problem gives you great insight into her methods for problem solving. If you want to learn about a developer's ability to apply lessons learned, ask what she would change given the chance to start her most recent project anew. Good developers are passionate about their work. Asking them about past experience will bring out that passion and tell you what correct answers to technical trivia questions cannot.

If you have been diligent in staffing a strong team, you want to do whatever is within your power to keep the team together. Retention factors such as compensation may be out of your hands, but make sure you're taking care of the little things that help to foster a healthy work environment. Good developers are often strongly motivated by recognition. Use this fact to your advantage and acknowledge stellar performances. Finding great developers is difficult; letting people know they are valued is not. Don't miss simple chances to build morale and boost productivity.

Be careful with negative reinforcement. Too much of it may stifle a developer's creativity and reduce productivity. Worse yet, it's likely to create dissension within the team. Good developers are smart; they know they're not wrong all of the time. If you're picking apart the minutiae of their work, you'll lose their respect. Keep criticism constructive and don't require that every solution look like it came from you.

The importance of staffing your development team correctly can't be overstated. These are the people who do the heavy lifting. When it comes to estimates, they're all treated as equal producers. Make sure it's tough to crack the starting lineup, and once you've got a winning team, go the extra mile to keep it together.

Author bio available on page 111.

Software Doesn't Really Exist

Chad LaVigne

SOFTWARE ENGINEERING IS OFTEN COMPARED to well-established disciplines such as civil engineering. There's a problem with these analogies; unlike the very tangible products created by these traditional practices, software doesn't really exist. Not in the traditional sense anyway. Those of us in the world of ones and zeros aren't constrained by the same physical rules that bind classic engineering paradigms. While applying engineering principles to the software design phase works well, assuming you can implement the design in the same manner used by more traditional engineering approaches is unrealistic.

Both business and software are living, moving entities. Business requirements change rapidly due to things like newly acquired business partners and marketing strategies. This makes it very difficult to approach a software project in the same manner as a traditional engineering pursuit such as bridge construction. It is highly unlikely that you'll be asked to move the location of a bridge halfway through a construction project. However, it is very likely that the acquisition of a business partner will require you to add support for organization-based content management to an application. This comparison should put things into perspective. We often say that software architecture decisions are difficult to change but not nearly so much as things that are literally and figuratively set in stone.

Knowing the products we build are pliable and that the requirements surrounding them are likely to change puts us in a different position than someone building an immovable object. Engineering endeavors of the physical flavor are much easier to implement in a "plan the work, work the plan" nature. With software, things need to be tackled in more of a "plan the work, massage the plan" fashion.

These differences aren't always bad news—at times they can be advantageous. For example, you're not necessarily constrained to building the components of a software system in a specific order so you can tackle high-risk issues first. This is in direct contrast to something like bridge construction, where there are many physical limitations surrounding the order in which tasks are accomplished.

However, the flexibility of software engineering does present some issues, many of which are self-imposed. As architects, we are very aware of the "soft" nature of our craft and we like to solve problems. Worse yet, the business owners are vaguely aware of these facts. This makes it easy for them to push big changes. Don't be too eager to accommodate large architectural changes just because it appeals to your solution-providing nature. Decisions like that can break an otherwise healthy project.

Remember that a requirements document is not a blueprint, and software doesn't really exist. The virtual objects that we create are easier to change than their physical-world counterparts, which is a good thing because many times they're required to. It's OK to plan as though we're building an immovable object; we just can't be surprised or unprepared when we're asked to move said object.

Author bio available on page 111.

Learn a New Language

Burkhardt Hufnagel

TO BE SUCCESSFUL AS AN ARCHITECT, you must be able to make yourself understood by people who don't speak your native tongue. No, I'm not suggesting you learn Esperanto or even Klingon, but you should at least speak basic Business, and Testing. And, if you aren't fluent in Programmer, you should make that a top priority.

If you don't see the value in learning other languages, consider the following scenario. The business people want a change made to an existing system, so they call a meeting with the architect and programmers to discuss it. Unfortunately, none of the technical team speaks Business and none of the business people speaks Programmer. The meeting will likely go something like this:

- A business person talks for a minute about the need for a relatively simple enhancement to an existing product, and explains how making the change will enable the sales team to increase both market and mind share.

- While the business person is still speaking, the architect starts sketching some kind of occult symbols on a notepad and enters into quiet argument with the one of the programmers in their strange multisyllabic tongue.

- Eventually the business person finishes and looks expectantly at the architect.

- After the whispered argument completes, the architect walks to the whiteboard and begins drawing several complex diagrams that are supposed to represent multiple views of the existing system while explaining (in complex technical terms) why the requested enhancement is virtually impossible without major changes and may actually require a complete redesign/rewrite of the entire system.

- The business people (who understood little of the diagram and less of the explanation) are openly stunned and find it hard to believe that something so simple would require such massive changes. They begin to wonder if the architect is serious or just making things up to avoid making the change.

- Meanwhile, the architect and programmers are just as surprised that the business people don't see how the "minor" change will require major modifications to the core system functionality.

And therein lies the problem. Neither group understands how the other thinks or what half of the words they use means. This leads to mistrust and miscommunication. It's a basic psychological principle that people are more comfortable with those who are similar to them than those who are different from them.

Imagine how the aforementioned scenario might change if the architect were able to explain the issues to the business folk in terms they understand and relay the business issues to the programmers in terms they understand. Instead of surprise and mistrust, the result would be agreement and approval.

I'm not saying that learning multiple languages will cure all your problems, but it will help prevent the miscommunications and misunderstandings that lead to problems.

For those of you who decide this makes sense, I wish you success on your journey. Or, as the Klingons say, *Qapla*!

Author bio available on page 175.

You Can't Future-Proof Solutions

Richard Monson-Haefel

Today's Solution Is Tomorrow's Problem

NO ONE CAN PREDICT THE FUTURE. If you accept this as a universal truth, then the question becomes, how far ahead is the future? One decade? Two years? Twenty minutes? If you can't predict the future, then you can't predict anything beyond right now. This very moment and the ones that preceded it are all you are know until the next moment occurs. This is the reason we have car accidents; if you knew you were going to have an accident on Thursday, you would probably stay home.

Yet we see software architects try to design systems that will be, for lack of a better term, "future-proof" all the time. It's simply not possible to future-proof an architecture. No matter what architectural decision you make now, that choice will become obsolete eventually. The cool programming language you used will eventually become the COBOL of tomorrow. Today's distributed framework will become tomorrow's DCOM. In short, today's solution will always be tomorrow's problem.

If you accept this fact—that the choices you make today will most certainly be wrong in the future—then it relieves you of the burden of trying to future-proof your architectures. If any choice you make today will be a bad choice in the future, then don't worry about what the future will hold—choose the best solution that meets your needs today.

One of the problems architects have today is analysis paralysis, and a big contribution to that problem is trying to guess the best technology for the future. Choosing a good technology for right now is hard enough; choosing one that will be relevant in the future is futile. Look at what your business needs now. Look at what the technology market offers now. Choose the best solution that meets your needs now, because anything else will not only be wrong choice tomorrow, but the wrong choice today.

Richard Monson-Haefel is an independent software developer who coauthored all five editions of Enterprise JavaBeans *and both editions of* Java Message Service *(all O'Reilly). He's a multitouch interface designer/developer and a leading expert on enterprise computing.*

The User Acceptance Problem

Norman Carnovale

PEOPLE AREN'T ALWAYS HAPPY about new systems or major upgrades. This can pose a threat to the successful completion of a project.

It's not uncommon for people to disagree with the decision to implement a new system—especially at the beginning. This should be expected, and the reasons noted. However, initial reactions to a new system are less of a concern than a sustained negative reaction.

Your goal as an architect is to be aware of and measure the threat of acceptance problems and work toward mitigating those threats. To do this you have to be cognizant of them and consider the reasons for them. Some of the more common reasons are:

- People may have concerns about the need for a new system (and subsequent retirement of an old system). This can also include fear of losing functionality or losing influence or power when roles change.

- People fear new (unproven) technology.

- People have cost/budget concerns.

- People simply do not like change.

Each of these reasons requires different possible solutions, some of which you can address and others you can't. You have to recognize the difference and deal quickly with those that you can. Start early having discussions with your end users about the new system and its real and perceived benefits and disadvantages. The most effective long-term solution is to use the design of the system itself to address the concerns. Other effective solutions include training, scheduled system demonstrations (early in the project lifecycle), and sharing knowledge of what users will get with a new system.

A "project champion" can help avoid user acceptance problems. Ideally this should be a person that represents the user group or stakeholders. This person sometimes has to be convinced himself. If there is none, then push for one from the very beginning. Once you've recruited a project champion, give him your assistance in every way you can.

Author bio available on page 43.

The Importance of Consommé

Eben Hewitt

A CONSOMMÉ IS AN EXTREMELY CLARIFIED BROTH, usually made with beef or veal, served as a delicate soup. A well-made consommé is perfectly clear. It is considered challenging and time-consuming to make, because there is only one way to remove the fat and other solids that cloud the broth and gain the absolute clarity the dish requires: repeated, simple, fine-grained straining. This straining again and again, this hyperconscious refining of the mixture, creates an intensely rich flavor. It's as if to taste a consommé is to taste the very essence of a thing. That is, in fact, the point of the dish.

In culinary schools in America, a simple test is administered to student chefs making consommé: the teacher drops a dime into your amber broth; if you can read the date on the dime resting at the bottom of the bowl, you pass. If you can't, you fail.

Software architecture requires a continual refinement of thought, a repeated straining of ideas until we have determined the essence of each requirement in the system. We ask, like Hamlet holding Yorick's skull, what is this thing? What are its properties? Its relations? We clarify our concepts, to make the relations within the architecture verifiably true, internally consistent.

Many missed requirements and bugs in software can be traced to ambiguous, general language. Ask customers, developers, analysts, and users the same questions repeatedly, until they are drowsy with boredom. Now disguise your question to pose it in a different way, like an attorney looking for a snag in the alibi, to tease out anything new, any differences or contradictions. Strain and strain again.

Focus on what can be removed from the concepts presented in the architecture, the nouns that compose them, to determine their essence. Bring surgical precision to the language you find in your requirements, rejecting ambiguity, generality, unwarranted assumptions, or extraneous verbiage. This serves to make your concepts richer, more robust. Reduce and reduce again.

Test statements by asking "Would you make the same statement if I appended 'always and forever and in every circumstance' to it?" People resist committing to absolutes like this, and must refine their words. Force representations of concepts through a linguistic sieve to clarify them. Do this again, until you are left with only the exhaustive list of simple and verifiably true statements that describe the essential nature of the system.

You'll know when the architecture is finished: when you can look through it and read the date on a dime.

Author bio available on page 161.

For the End User, the Interface Is the System

Vinayak Hegde

THERE ARE TOO MANY GOOD PRODUCTS hidden behind bad user-interfaces. The end user will access the system through its user interface. If the quality of the user's experience while interacting with your product suffers, then his impression of your product will suffer, no matter how technologically advanced and path-breaking your product might be.

The user interface is an important component of architecture and an often-neglected one. The architect should enlist the services of specialists such as user experience designers and usability experts. The user interaction experts, along with the architect, can drive the interface design as well as its coupling with the internal mechanisms. Involving user interface experts at an early stage and throughout the product development phases ensures that the final product is polished, and that the integration of the user interface with the product is seamless. The architect should also look at doing user interaction testing while the product is still in beta with actual end users, and incorporate their feedback into the final product.

Often the usage of a product changes over time as technology changes and features are added. The architect should ensure that user interface changes with the architecture reflect the expectations of the users.

User interactions should be one of the goals of the complete product architecture. In fact, user interaction should be an integral part of the decision-making process for architecture tradeoffs and internal product documentation as much as robustness and performance. Changes in user interaction design should be captured over time, just like code. This is especially true in products where the user interface is written in a different programming language than the rest of the product.

It is the architect's responsibility to make the most common interactions not only easy but also rewarding for the end user. Better user interfaces lead to happier customers , which helps improve customer productivity. If your product helps people become more productive, then it will contribute to the business's bottom-line.

Vinayak Hegde is a geek interested in computers, photography, and entrepreneurship. He is currently working as an architect with Akamai Technologies.

Great Software Is Not Built, It Is Grown

Bill de hÓra

AS AN ARCHITECT, you are tasked with providing the initial structure and arrangement of software systems that will grow and change over time, will have to be reworked, and will have to talk to other systems—and almost always in ways you and your stakeholders did not foresee. Even though we are called *architects*, and we borrow many metaphors from building and engineering, great software is not built, it is grown.

The single biggest predictor of software failure is size; on reflection there's almost no benefit to be had from starting with a large system design. Yet at some point we will all be tempted to do exactly that. As well as being prone to incidental complexity and inertia, designing large systems upfront means larger projects, which are more likely to fail, more likely to be untestable, more likely to be fragile, more likely to have unneeded and unused parts, more likely to be expensive, and more likely to have a negative political dimension.

Therefore resist trying to design a large complete system to "meet or exceed" the known requirements and desired properties, no matter how tempting that might be. Have a grand vision, but not a grand design. Let you and your system learn to adapt as the situation and requirements inevitably change.

How to do this? The best way to ensure that a software system can evolve and adapt is to evolve and adapt it from the very outset. Inducing a system to evolve means starting with a small running system, a working subset of the intended architecture—the simplest thing that could possibly work. This nascent system will have many desirable properties and can teach us much about the architecture that a large system, or worse, a collection of architectural documents, never can. You are more likely to have been involved in its implementation. Its lack of surface area will be easier to test and therefore less prone to coupling. It will require a smaller team, which will reduce the cost of coordinating the project. Its properties will be easier to observe. It will be easier to deploy. It will teach you and your team at the earliest possible moment what does and does not work. It will tell you where the system will not evolve easily, where it is likely to crystallize, where it is fragile. Where it might break. Perhaps most important, it will be comprehensible and tangible to its stakeholders from the beginning, allowing them to grow into the overall design as well.

Design the smallest system you can, help deliver it, and let it evolve toward the grand vision. Although this might feel like giving up control, or even shirking your responsibilities, ultimately your stakeholders will thank you for it. Do not confuse an evolutionary approach with throwing requirements out, the dreaded phasing, or building one to throw away.

Author bio available on page 117.

Index

Colophon

The cover and heading font is Gotham; the text font is Minion Pro.

Try the online edition free for 45 days

Get the information you need when you need it, with Safari Books Online. Safari Books Online contains the complete version of the print book in your hands plus thousands of titles from the best technical publishers, with sample code ready to cut and paste into your applications.

Safari is designed for people in a hurry to get the answers they need so they can get the job done. You can find what you need in the morning, and put it to work in the afternoon. As simple as cut, paste, and program.

To try out Safari and the online edition of the **above title** FREE for 45 days, go to www.oreilly.com/go/safarienabled and enter the coupon code HWIGKEH.

To see the complete Safari Library visit:
safari.oreilly.com